Thomas Hutchins

An Historical Narrative and Topographical Description of

Louisiana and West-Florida,

comprehending the river Mississippi with its principal branches and

settlementss, and the rivers Pearl, Pascagoula

Thomas Hutchins

An Historical Narrative and Topographical Description of Louisiana and West-Florida,
comprehending the river Mississippi with its principal branches and settlementss, and the rivers Pearl, Pascagoula

ISBN/EAN: 9783337377205

Printed in Europe, USA, Canada, Australia, Japan

Cover: Foto ©ninafisch / pixelio.de

More available books at **www.hansebooks.com**

A N

HISTORICAL NARRATIVE

AND

TOPOGRAPHICAL DESCRIPTION

OF

LOUISIANA,

AND

WEST-FLORIDA,

COMPREHENDING THE

RIVER MISSISSIPPI WITH ITS PRINCIPAL BRANCHES
AND SETTLEMENTS, AND THE RIVERS PEARL,
PASCAGOULA, MOBILLE, PERDIDO,
ESCAMBIA, CHACTA-HATCHA, &c.

THE

CLIMATE, SOIL, AND PRODUCE

WHETHER

ANIMAL, VEGETABLE, OR MINERAL;

WITH

Directions for Sailing into all the Bays, Lakes, Harbours and Rivers on
the North Side of the Gulf of Mexico, and for Navigating between the
Islands fituated along that Coaft, and afcending the Miffiffippi River.

By THOMAS HUTCHINS,
GEOGRAPHER TO THE UNITED STATES.

PHILADELPHIA:

PRINTED FOR THE AUTHOR, AND SOLD BY ROBERT
AITKEN, NEAR THE COFFEE-HOUSE, IN
MARKET-STREET.
M.DCC.LXXXIV.

THE

P R E F A C E.

SEVERAL years residence in the Province of West-Florida, during which I entered into a minute examination of its coasts, harbours, lakes, and rivers, having made me perfectly acquainted with their situation, bearings, soundings, and every particular requisite to be known by Navigators, for their benefit I am induced to make my observations public. The expence and trouble at which this knowledge has been acquired, are far from inconsiderable; however, if the accurate surveys and descriptions I am thereby enabled to give, prove instructive and beneficial to my country, I shall esteem myself amply repaid.

It may be proper to observe that I have had the assistance of the remarks and surveys, so far as relates to the mouths of the Mississippi and the coast and soundings of West-Florida, of the late ingenious Mr. George Gauld, a Gentleman who was employed by the Lords of the British Admiralty for the express purpose of making an accurate chart of the abovementioned places.

I have also had recourse, in describing some parts of the Mississippi, to the publication of Captain Pitman, who resided many years on that river, and was well acquainted with the country through which it flows.

A particular detail of the advantages that may in time accrue to the possessors of West-Florida, with a complete description of the country and its productions,
would

would not make an improper addition to the following work; but as the more immediate purpose of it is to point out the dangers of its coasts to the approaching mariner, I shall confine the cursory remarks I make on those heads, to such particulars only as are most deserving of notice.

Before I enter on the prosecution of my design, I would just observe, that I shall be more solicitous to make the result of my investigations useful than amusing, I shall endeavour rather to be clear and intelligible than study to deliver myself in florid language.

AN
HISTORICAL
AND
TOPOGRAPHICAL
DESCRIPTION, &c.

A DESCRIPTION of the river Miffiffippi and the country through which it flows, called Louifiana, would have been the firft objects fubmitted to the reader's attention; were it not humbly prefumed that a fhort account of the difcovery of the river Miffiffippi, and a view of the different States to which its banks have been fubjected are judged neceffary, before their defcription is attempted.

The merit of firft difcovering the river Miffiffippi, Difcovery of the Miffiffippi. (or in the language of the natives, Mefchafipi, for the general appellation of the former is a corruption of the latter) according to Lewis Hennepin's account publifhed in London 1698, is due to the Sieur la Salle, who difcovered that river in 1682. It feems that father Hennepin forgot that this river was previoufly difcovered by Ferdinand de Soto in 1541, alfo by Col. Wood in 1654, and by Captain Bolt in 1670. Monfieur de la Salle was the firft who traverfed that Arrival and murder of la Salle. river. In the fpring of the fame year 1682, he paffed down to the mouths of the Miffiffippi; he afterwards remounted that river, and returned to Canada in the month of October following, from whence he took his paffage to France, where he gave fo flattering an account of the advantages that would certainly accrue from the fettling a colony in thofe parts, that a company was formed for carrying thofe defigns into execution, with a fquadron confifting of four veffels; having

having on board a fufficient number of perfons, and
all kinds of goods and provifions, neceffary for the
fervice of the new colony, which he propofed to fix
at or near the mouth of the Miffiffippi. But having
failed beyond the mouth of the river, he attempted
to fix a colony at the bay of St. Bernard, where he arrived the 18th of February 1684, about 100 leagues
weftward of the Miffiffippi. There his men under-
went fuch hardfhips that moft of them perifhed mife-
rably. The leader, animated with an ardent defire of
extending (his difcoveries, made various excurfions
with fuch of them who were able to travel; but on the
19th of March 1687, two of his men villainoufly mur-
dered him, when exploring the interior parts of the
country, in fearch of mines, and of the tract which
led to thofe of St. Barbe in New Mexico.

About feven years after, Monf. Ibberville, a refpect-
able officer in the French navy, undertook to execute
whatever La Salle had promifed; and his reputation
being eftablifhed already, the court intrufted him with
the conduct of the project. He carried his people
very fafely to the mouth of the great river, and there
laid the foundation of the firft colony the French
ever had in the Miffiffippi. He took care to provide
them with every thing neceffary for their fubfiftance,
and obliged them to erect a fort, for their defence
againft the Indians. This being done, he returned to
France in order to obtain fupplies.

The fuccefs of his voyage made him extremely
welcome at court, and he was foon in a condition to
put to fea again. His fecond voyage was as fortunate
as the firft; but very unluckily for his colony, he
died whilft he was preparing for the third. The defign might have been abandoned, had not Crozat, a
private man of an immenfe fortune, undertaken its
fupport at his own expence. In 1712, the King gave
him Louifiana. Thus Lewis imitated the Pope,
who

who divided between the kings of Spain and Portugal the territories of America, where the holy fee had not one inch of ground.

In this grant the bounds are fixed by the Illinois river and the lake of that name on the North; by Carolina on the Eaſt, the gulph of Mexico on the South, and New Mexico on the Weſt. As to Canada, or New France, the French court would ſcarcely admit it had any other northern boundary than the Pole. The avidity of Great Britain was equal, but France having been unfortunate in the war of 1710, the northern boundary of Canada was fixed by the treaty of Utrecht in 1713. It aſſigns New Britain and Hudſon's Bay, on the North of Canada, to Great Britain; and commiſſioners afterwards on both ſides aſcertained the limits by an imaginary line, running from a cape or promontory in New Britain to the Atlantic ocean, in 58 degrees 30 minutes North latitude, thence Southweſt to the lake Miſgoſink or Miſtaſim; from thence farther South-weſt directly to the latitude of 49 degrees. All the lands to the North of the imaginary line, being aſſigned to Great Britain; and all ſouthward of that line, as far as the river of St. Laurence, to the French. Theſe were at that time the true limits of Louiſiana and Canada, Crozat's grant not ſubſiſting long after the death of Lewis XIV.

In order to have ſome plauſible pretence for ſetting on foot a project for changing the face of public affairs in France, this ſettlement was thought the moſt convenient; and therefore all imaginable pains were taken to repreſent it as a paradiſe, and place from whence inexhauſtible riches might be derived, provided due encouragement could be obtained from government. For this purpoſe it was thought requiſite that a new company ſhould be erected, to make way for which Mr. Crozat was to reſign his grant; which he did accordingly.

Bounds of Louiſiana.

Limits of Louiſiana and Canada by the treaty of Utrecht.

Crozat's grant vacated.

This

This occafioned the noife that was made about the Miffiffippi, not in France only, but throughout all Europe, which was filled with romantic ftories of the vaft fruitfulnefs of the banks of this great river, and the incredible wealth that was likely to flow from thence; and thofe accounts, though true in part, in the end proved ruinous to many.

Bounds of Louifiana before the peace of 1762.

Before the treaty of peace in 1762, Louifiana, or the fouthern part of New France, extended in the French maps from the gulph of Mexico, in about 29 degrees, to near 45 degrees of North latitude, on the Weft of the Miffiffippi, and to near 39 degrees on its eaftern bank. Its boundaries were Canada on the North; New York, Pennfylvania, Maryland, Virginia, North and South Carolina, Georgia, and the North-weft part of the eafternmoft peninfula of Florida, on the Eaft; the Gulf of Mexico on the South; and laftly the kingdom of New Mexico on the Weft.

Abfurd claims.

The European ftates having obferved that kings and republicks claimed the fovereignty of every tract which had been feen, and were pretended to have been difcovered by navigators failing under their flags, their geographers were not permitted to publifh maps which might have contradicted fuch wild claims. This was the abfurdity of former days. But political circumftances often emboldened pretenders to urge their chimerical rights; and their no lefs chimerical opponents then yielded what they had no better right to cede. But the abfurd recognition of fuch abfurd pretenfions is but a temporary compliance. It ever did and ever will fow the feeds of implacable animofities and contentions, until pre-occupancy and cultivation, the true tefts of lawful poffeffion, fhall have remedied the former invalidity of the claim.

Both fides of the Miffiffippi continued under the dominion of his moft Chriftian Majefty till the peace of 1762, when the eaftern fide was ceded to the king of

Great

Great Britain by the 7th article of the definitive treaty, in the following words. " In order to re-eftablifh peace on folid and durable foundations, and to re- Divifion line between the French and Englifh in 1762. move for ever all fubject of difpute with regard to the limits of the Britifh and French territories on the continent of America, it is agreed, that for the future, the confines between the dominions of his Britannic Majefty, in that part of the world, fhall be fixed irrevocably by a line drawn along the middle of the river Miffiffippi, from its fource to the river Ibberville, and from thence, by a line drawn along the middle of this river, and the Lakes Maurepas and Ponchartrain, to the fea ; and for this purpofe the moft Chriftian King cedes in full right, and guaranties to his Britannic Majefty, the river and port of the Mobille, and every thing which he poffeffes, or ought to poffefs, on the left fide of the river Miffiffippi, except the town of New Orleans, and the ifland in which it is fituated, which fhall remain to France; provided that the navigation of the river Miffiffippi fhall be equally free, as well to the fubjects of Great Britain, as to thofe of France, in its whole length, from its fource to the fea, and exprefly that part which is between the faid ifland of New Orleans, and the right bank of that river, as well as the paffage both in and out of its mouth: it is further ftipulated that the veffels belonging to the fubjects of either nation, fhall not be ftopped, vifited, or fubjected to the payment of any duty whatfoever. The ftipulations inferted in the 4th article, in favour of the inhabitants of Canada, fhall alfo take place with regard to the inhabitants of the countries ceded by this article."

In the year 1762, and the day before the preli- The ceffion of his Chriftian Majefty to Spain. minary articles to the peace were figned, his Chriftian Majefty ceded to Spain all his territories on the weftern fide of the Miffiffippi, together with the town of

B   New

New Orleans, and the peninfula in which it is fituated on the eaftern bank. But the inhabitants of Louifiana were ignorant of this ceffion before the year 1764, when Mr. D'Abbadie, then governor, publifhed the king's letter to him on that fubject, mentioning the date of the ceffion, and containing a declaration that he had ftipulated with Spain that the French laws and ufages fhould not be altered.

Bounds by the Definitive Treaty of 1783. The definitive treaty, between Great-Britain and the United States of America, figned at Paris the 3d day of September 1783, runs as follows:

"ARTICLE 1. His Britannic Majefty acknowledges the faid United States, viz. New-Hampfhire, Maffachufetts-Bay, Rhode-Ifland and Providence Plantations, Connecticut, New-York, New-Jerfey, Pennfylvania, Delaware, Maryland, Virginia, North-Carolina, South-Carolina, and Georgia, to be free, fovereign, and independent ftates; that he treats with them as fuch, and for himfelf, his heirs and fucceffors, relinquifhes all claims to the government, property, and territorial rights of the fame, and every part thereof.

"ART. 2. And that all difputes which might arife in future, on the fubject of the boundaries of the faid United States, may be prevented, it is hereby agreed and declared, that the following are and fhall be their boundaries, viz. From the North-weft angle of Nova-Scotia, viz. that angle which is formed by a line drawn due North from the fource of St. Croix river to the Highlands, along the faid Highlands, which divide thofe rivers that empty themfelves into the river St. Laurence from thofe which fall into the Atlantic ocean, to the North-weftermoft head of Connecticut river; thence down along the middle of that river to the forty-fifth degree of North latitude; from thence by a line due Weft on faid latitude, until it ftrikes the river Irriquois or Cataraqui; thence along the

the middle of the faid river into Lake Ontario; through the middle of the faid lake until it ftrikes the communication by water between that lake and Lake Erie ; thence along the middle of faid communication into Lake Erie, through the middle of faid lake, until it arrives at the water communication between that lake and Lake Huron, thence through the middle of faid lake to the water communication between that lake and Lake Superior ; thence through Lake Superior, northward of the Ifles Royal and Phelipeaux to the Long Lake ; thence through the middle of faid Long Lake and the water communication between it and the Lake of the Woods, to the faid Lake of the Woods, thence through the faid Lake to the moft North-weftern point thereof, and from thence on a due Weft courfe to the river Mifliffippi; thence by a line to be drawn along the middle of the faid river Mifliffippi; thence by a line to be drawn along the middle of the faid river Mifliffippi until it fhall inter-fect the northernmoft part of the thirty-firft degree of North latitude. South, by a line to be drawn due Eaft from the determination of the line laft mention-ed in the latitude of thirty-one degrees North of the Equator, to the middle of the river Apalachicola or Catanouche: thence along the middle thereof to its junction with the Flint-River: thence ftraight to the head of St. Mary's River: and thence down along the middle of St. Mary's River to the Atlantic ocean: Eaft, by a line to be drawn along the middle of the River St. Croix, from its mouth in the Bay of Fundy to its fource, and from its fource directly North to the aforefaid Highlands which divide the rivers that fall into the Atlantic ocean from thofe which fall into the River St. Laurence, comprehending all iflands within twenty leagues of any part of the fhores of the United States, and lying between lines to be drawn due Eaft from the points where the aforefaid
boundaries

boundaries between Nova-Scotia on the one part, and Eaſt-Florida on the other, ſhall reſpectively touch the Bay of Fundy and the Atlantic ocean, excepting ſuch iſlands as now are or heretofore have been within the limits of the ſaid province of Nova-Scotia.

" ART. 8. The navigation of the river Miſſiſſippi, from its ſource to the ocean, ſhall for ever remain free and open to the ſubjects of Great Britain, and the citizens of the United States."

Having mentioned all the boundaries that were at different periods aſſigned to Louiſiana, the conduct of the Spaniards on poſſeſſing themſelves of that colony, is to be conſidered next in courſe.

Arrival of Don Ulloa at New Orleans with ſoldiers.

Don Antonio Ulloa arrived at New Orleans about the middle of the year 1766, but deferred to take poſſeſſion of the government of the colony in his Catholic Majeſty's name, until he had received ſpecial orders to that effect.

In the beginning of the year 1767, two thouſand Spaniſh ſoldiers were ſent from the Havanna, but he did not then take poſſeſſion of the country. He ſent however about ſixty of theſe troops to erect two forts, one oppoſite to the Britiſh fort, named Bute, on the mouth of the Ibberville, and the other on the weſtern ſide of the Miſſiſſippi, a little below the Natchez, where a detachment of Britiſh troops had taken poſt; another party was ſent in the autumn of 1767 to build a fort at the mouth of the river Miſſouri; but the commandant had poſitive orders not to interfere with the civil government of the Illinois country, where Monſ. de Saint Ange the French commandant continued to command with about twenty French ſoldiers. Don Antonio Ulloa, without taking poſſeſſion in his Catholic Majeſty's name, and conſequently without authority from France or Spain, eſtabliſhed monopolies, reſtricted commerce, and committed ſeveral abuſes, which rendered him odious

to

to the colonifts. At laft, on the 29th of October 1768, the council iffued a decree to oblige him and the principal Spanifh officers to leave the province in November following, notwithftanding M. Aubry's remonftrances, and the proteft he made againft the edict of the council. Spaniards obliged to depart from Louifiana.

Don Ulloa's conduct had rendered him the more obnoxious, as, from the letter written by the king of France, acquainting Mr. D'Abbadie with the ceffion he had made to Spain, it appeared that the two kings had agreed, that Louifiana fhould retain her laws, privileges and cuftoms. The French, nay the Spaniards themfelves, all blamed Mr. Aubry's acquiefcence; for every one was fenfible that the king of France never would have directed him to treat Don Ulloa with an obfequioufnefs which degraded royal authority and the French nation; and that his inftructions could, at moft, authorife Mr. Aubry to follow that officer's advice, until the government of Louifiana fhould be delivered to Spain. Whatever entreaties had been ufed to perfuade Don Ulloa to take poffeffion, and by that meafure render the exercife of his authority lawful, he evaded, but did not ceafe to opprefs; fo that he loft the efteem which he had acquired by the publication of his voyages; and the colonifts having been informed of the feverity with which he had governed the city of Quito in Peru, he was only confidered as a tyrant, whofe fole merit was to be learned in the mathematics. Don Ulloa obnoxious to the people.

The fuperior council, guided by the Intendant and the Attorney General, having threatened him with a profecution, he declared that, at the Balize, Mr. Aubry had privately delivered to him the command of the colony. As none could conceive that a clandeftine poffeffion ought to authorife the public exercife of fovereign power, Ulloa's declaration was judged an artifice of the groffeft texture; and Mr. Aubry, Threatened with a profecution.

who

who affirmed the declaration to be true, was not believed. It made him fall into contempt, and emboldened the leaders of the party which oppofed him. Thefe

increafed the doubts of the public relative to the ceffion, and ferved to convince every one, that the Spaniards did not ferioufly intend taking poffeffion :---
" The ceffion," faid they, " was made in 1762, the
" day before the preliminary articles of peace were
" figned : near two years elapfed before it was firft
" known by the king's letter to Mr. D'Abbadie :
" more than another year paffed before the arrival of
" Don Ulloa, who has been above two years in the
" country and did not yet take poffeffion." If the reflections occafioned by thefe circumftances put together ; if the conjectures fcattered in the Englifh news-papers, or by the Englifh who came into the country, led the inhabitants to think that the ceffion was fictitious, and a ftate manœuvre, their fears were at the fame time quieted, fince they did not apprehend thofe evils which the change of fovereignty makes almoft unavoidable, even when the new government is milder and more favourable. On the other hand, their indignation was the greater againft Don Ulloa, who abufed the reafons of ftate that were fuppofed to be the caufe of his having been fent to Louifiana ; who availed himfelf of Mr. Aubry's imbecility, to eftablifh a fpecies of defpotifm, the more intolerant, as it fhocked the manners of the French nation.

To put a ftop to this tyranny, it would have been fufficient to commence, with circumfpection, a juridical profecution againft him, and inform the miniftry of the proceedings. But the council began by iffuing a decree for expelling him and the Spaniards. To reduce the people to the neceffity of fupporting that violence, the leaders excited them to offend the king of Spain, from whom they had received no injury, and who doubtlefs would have punifhed his officer,

ficer, had the council proceeded with refpect, and ufed lawful means to tranfmit to him their grievances. But, indignities were offered to the Spanifh flag; a ftep which rendered the infult perfonal to the king of Spain, and made him overlook his envoy's mifde-meanors. This is not all : the council and the inha-bitants fent deputies to France, charged them to re- prefent the grievances of the colony to their fovereign, and fupplicate him to retain the province. Their prayers were accompanied with proteftations of devo-tion and loyalty. But before the departure of thefe deputies, the leaders of the faction feduced fome members of the council, fecretly fent another depu-tation to Penfacola ; and, without the people's know-ledge, offered Louifiana to Great Britain !

The dread of being called to account, with which the crafty Don Ulloa had often threatened the Intendant and the Attorney General, that he might obftruct their profecutions, and filence them, relative-ly to his own conduct, was doubtlefs the fole caufe of that defperate ftep, the authors of which might have forefeen the unfuccefsful iffue, had they not been bereft of their fenfes. It is true that there has been no public inquiry on that head ; and therefore, the public has no juridical proof of this fact ; but the characteriftics of fuch inquiry as was made, its terri-fying apparatus, its refult, and the concerted filence of thofe by whom it was directed, fufficiently confirm not only what is openly faid among the Englifh, but what the inhabitants of Louifiana whifper to each other, when complaining of their miferies with which the perfidioufnefs of their leaders had loaded them, though not accomplices of their crimes. It is alfo faid, that the governor of Weft-Florida was unwil-ling to countenance the treafon and revolt of the fub-jects of a prince then in peace with Great Britain : it is affirmed that he fent to Mr. Aubry the original

offers

offers he had received, and that Don Ulloa, who had not yet failed, carried them with him to Europe for his juftification. Why then did not Mr. Aubry produce that paper to confound the confpirators ? They would have been looked upon with execration by the people whom they had betrayed, and the difturbances would have immediately fubfided. Can it be believed, that the governor of Florida infifted on fecrecy, as it is intimated by fome perfons who would be glad to apologize for Mr. Aubry's conduct refpecting this matter ? Had the inteftine divifions, which then rent the Britifh colonies of North-America, induced the Britifh governor to difcover the confpiracy in order to prevent the fatal confequences of fo dangerous an example, would not fecrecy have deprived him of the only fruit he could expect from his policy ?

—Never heard of.

Monfieur de Sacier, one of the council, with two other Gentlemen of the colony, who were fent to France with the edict of the fuperior council, and to implore the protection of the king, as before mentioned, were imprifoned on their arrival, and have never been heard of fince.

Gen. O'Riley's arrival at the Balize.

During fix months, which elapfed before news could be received from Europe, the unhappy colonifts vainly flattered themfelves with hopes of being juftified for the fteps they had taken by the court of France. On the 23d of July 1769, news was brought to New Orleans of the arrival of General O'Riley at the Balize, with eighteen tranfports, followed by ten more from the Havanna, having four thoufand five hundred troops on board, and loaded with ftores and ammunition. This intelligence threw the town into the greateft confternation and perplexity, as but a few days before, letters had arrived from Europe fignifying that the colony was reftored to France.

Inhabitants determined to oppofe him.

In the general diftraction that took place, the inhabitants of the town and the adjacent plantations determined

determined to oppofe the landing of the Spaniards, and fent couriers requiring the Germans and Acadian Neutrals to join them. On the 24th an exprefs arrived from General O'Riley, which was read by Monfieur Aubry to the people in church; by this they were informed that he was fent by his Catholic Majefty to take poffeffion of the colony, but not to diftrefs the inhabitants; and that when he fhould be in poffeffion, he would publifh the remaining part of the orders he had in charge from the king his mafter; and fhould any attempt be made to oppofe his landing, he was refolved not to depart until he could put his majefty's commands in execution.

The people, diffatisfied with this ambiguous meffage, Deputies fent to meet him. came to a refolution of fending three deputies to General O'Riley, viz. Meffieurs Grandmaifon town-major, La Friniere attorney-general, and De Mazant formerly captain in the colony's troops, and a man of very confiderable property; thefe gentlemen acquainted him, that the inhabitants had come to a refolution of abandoning the province, and demanded no other favour than that he would grant them two years to remove themfelves and effects. The general received the deputies with great politenefs, but did not enter into the merits of their embaffy, farther than affuring them, that he would comply with every reafonable requeft of the colonifts; that he had the intereft of their country much at heart, and nothing on his part fhould be wanting to promote it; that all paft tranfactions fhould be buried in oblivion, and all who had offended fhould be forgiven: to this he added every thing that he imagined could flatter the expectations of the people. On the firft of Auguft the deputies returned, and made public the kind reception the general had given them, and the fair promifes he had made. The minds of the people were now greatly tranquilized, and thofe who had before determined

C   fuddenly

suddenly to quit their plantations now refolved to remain until their crops were off the ground.

His arrival & difembarking of the troops at New Orleans.

On the 16th of Auguft 1769, General O'Riley with the frigate, tranfports and troops on board arrived oppofite to New Orleans. On the 18th the troops difembarked, and the general took poffeffion in form, of New Orleans and the province of Louifiana, in the name of his Catholic Majefty, as quietly as a French governor would have done in the happieft times; and on the 25th, ordered the attorney general and twelve others amongft the principal inhabitants to be arrefted.

Attorney-General and others arrefted.

Of thefe thirteen, no more than one was releafed: this was the printer, who produced the pofitive orders which the intendant had given him, for printing the decree iffued againft Don Ulloa, and feveral other writings. A few days before the proceedings began, a young gentleman nearly related to the attorney general, and one of the prifoners, feigned a defign of forcibly refcuing himfelf from the foldiers who guarded him. He received feveral wounds, which gave him that death which he fought. The proceedings againft the eleven others, were conducted in a military manner by Gen. O'Riley, and the members of the court were moftly Spanifh officers. The council of war pronounced their fentence on thofe proceedings. In vain did the attorney general and the other prifoners demand to be tried by the French laws. Thefe would not have proved favourable to their accufers. General O'Riley was fo unjuft as to refufe that reafonable requeft. The attorney general and four others, who were fhot with him, died with fortitude. Had they really deferved that fate, their condemnation is not the lefs criminal, in the eyes of thofe who are not ftupid enough to reverence authority when trampling upon the laws. The fentence of the court martial difhonours the authors and tools of that injuftice; it difhonours no others. The

Sentence of the Council of War.

The fix other ftate prifoners were fent to fort Mo-
ro in the ifland of Cuba, whence they were releafed
after one year's confinement. The eftates of the
eleven perfons, who were condemned by the court
martial, were confifcated, according to the practice
of moft countries; a practice as impolitic as it is
unjuft. It reflects difgrace on princes, occafions the
impunity of the greateft crimes, and often multiplies
the number of criminals. Many might be virtuous
enough not to fkreen a guilty kinfman from juftice;
but few have fufficient magnanimity to fee with indif-
ference the eftate of that kinfman pafs into the
prince's coffers, or thofe of his minifters. How many has not this fole reafon feduced to engage in
confpiracies or rebellions, which they would otherwife have wifhed to deftroy : in fuch cafes it frequently
happens that the prince, whom confifcations caufe to
behold as an enemy, is defervedly oppofed for his ra-
pacioufnefs or inattention to his own intereft.

The French beheld, with horror, their countrymen
given up to foreigners, privately tried and arbitrarily
punifhed, for crimes of which they were accufed in
a country fubject to France. The indignity offered
to Spain was the oftenfible caufe of their condemnation; but whatever their crime might have been,
France alone ought to have had cognizance of it. If
the accufed were guilty of nothing elfe; or if, for
ftate reafons, it was thought proper to mention that
offence only, the king of Spain would have caufed
his name to be for ever bleffed in the colony, had he,
a judge in his own caufe, generoufly forgiven. The
meafures that have been adopted, have produced a
very different effect. They are nearly the fame as
thofe of the Portuguefe government, which contrived
Father Malagrida's being burnt by the inquifition, on
the pretence of his having boafted that he had fometimes converfed with the Holy Virgin; but whofe

The French beheld, with horror, their countrymen given up to foreigners.

real

real crime was an attempt againſt his ſovereign's life, in order to make another family aſcend the throne. Crimes like theſe, openly perpetrated by the adminiſtration againſt the laws, common ſenſe and public ſafety ; can no where be palliated with the pretence of neceſſity. Whatever thoſe who adviſe them may think on the ſubject, they betray their country and their ſovereign himſelf. In free ſtates, where the perſonal ſafety of the meaneſt individual is as intereſting to the whole nation as that of the greateſt, crimes of this kind are never ſeen. They can be committed in ſuch countries only, where deſpotiſm is eſtabliſhed ; where a few, favoured ſlaves, reduce the reſt ſecretly to wiſh for the annihilation of thoſe whom they ſeemingly adore.

The ſame diſordered brains which projected the illegal proſecutions carried on againſt the factious leaders of Louiſiana, have doubtleſs fancied, that they would deſerve immortality for a maſterly ſtroke of policy, when they procured the abolition of the laws, privileges, and ſuperior council of Louiſiana, under the pretence of a decree iſſued againſt Don Ulloa. Have they really thought that people could be deceived by names which were to repreſent nothing ? The ſhadow of a tribunal. was eſtabliſhed under the name of Cabildo government, that is civil government, but the governor and his aſſeſſor are in fact the only judges. Since the judgments given by them jointly have the ſame virtue as thoſe of that Cabildo government, few are ſo unſkilful as to apply to this tribunal. Nay, who would dare to do it except in trifling matters? Was it likewiſe believed that, for the governor and his aſſeſſor's conveniency, the ſubſtituting of the Spaniſh language to the French, in all the juridical proceedings of Louiſiana, where the inhabitants underſtand the French language only; the impartial diſpenſation of juſtice, which is the true glory of the ſtate, would

Abolition of the laws of Louiſiana.

would thence be effectually promoted? Things will certainly go well, as long as governors and their affessors shall have all the qualifications that perfect judges ought to have, and whilst the parties can procure faithful interpreters: but it is as true that, wife as thefe regulations are boafted to be, they depopulate the colony.

General O'Riley confirmed all the decrees of the fuperior council, except that which had been iffued againft Don Ulloa. This was folemnly approving the feditious nomination of the members of Mr. Foucault's and the Attorney-General's making; it was therefore arrogantly annulling the proteft which Mr. Aubry had entered in behalf of the king of France and the public, againft that nomination, and all the decrees iffued out of that tribunal during the anarchy; it was depriving thofe who had been oppreffed from the hopes of obtaining redrefs in the colony. For, the council being abolifhed, how could any one take the benefit of the French laws, (fince trials by peers or juries are difufed) or think defpotic rulers would allow of applying to fovereign courts for obtaining new trials of the caufes, which they themfelves may have tried illegally, or againft evidence? But, to flatter the Spaniards, Gen. O'Riley had determined that they alone fhould be judges; and military men of that nation could not, with the leaft plaufibility, pretend that they were acquainted with the French laws; he, therefore, had rather cut off than untie. Such is the difpofition of tyrants of every rank and denomination: Alexander cutting the Gordian Knot is, perhaps, of all the fables that are confounded with hiftory, that which more truly characterifes defpotifm. Men who led by avarice and ambition obtain admittance to that order, difregarding the people to whofe prefervation they feem to have profeffedly devoted themfelves, but who are determined on making their fortunes, are never

Gen. O'Riley confirms the decrees of the Superior Council.

The difpofition of tyrants.

disturbed

difturbed in the leaft about the means which can promote their grand defign. Their eyes being fixed on
all thofe who have a fhare in the difpenfation of
wealth and honours, they fee them only. Their
mercenary zeal prompts them to wifh for their being
entrufted with iniquitous and inhuman orders, which
they alone are fit to execute. Strangers to nature,
they are deaf to the voice of juftice and the cries
of humanity ; and, unable to rife by noble and gene-
rous actions, they glory in difplaying their zeal for
the prince, by wholly loading themfelves with that
public execration which attends the execution of fan-
guinary orders. It is not from fuch abject fouls that
a prince, inebriated with power, can ever learn that
there are moments, not numerous indeed, but yet
frequent enough to comfort the oppreffed and cha-
ftife the oppreffor----moments, when, after having
made himfelf odious to his fubjects ; after having
weakened and degraded them, he may regret their
attachment, the courage which defpotifm has endeavoured to enervate, and the patriotifm which it has
attempted to deftroy.

Galvez takes
poffeffion of
the Britifh
pofts.

After this General Galvez Governor of New Orleans, in the year 1779, poffeffed himfelf of the Britifh pofts at the Ibberville and Baton Rouge. By ca-
pitulation, the poft at the Natchez was evacuated, and
the garrifon permitted to join the troops at Penfacola.
The Spaniards likewife reduced the forts of Mobille
and Penfacola ; the former in the year 1780, and
the latter in 1781. The above conquefts not only
fubjected the eaftern fide of the Miffiffippi, but the
whole province of Weft-Florida to the dominion of
Spain.

Having briefly touched on the principal revoluti-
ons which have happened in Louifiana, I fhall now
proceed with a fhort account of the Miffiffippi.

The fafety and commercial profperity which may
be

be fecured to the United States by the definitive trea- *Commercial advantages from the treaty of peace.*
ty of peace, will chiefly depend upon the fhare of
the navigation of the Miffiffippi which fhall be allowed to them. Is it not amazing, true as it is, that few
amongft us know this to be the key to the northern
part of the weftern continent? It is the only channel *Account of the Miffiffippi.*
through which that extenfive region, bathed by its
waters, and enriched by the many ftreams it receives,
communicates with the fea. And here let us further
obferve, that the Miffiffippi river may truly be confidered as the great paffage made by the hand of nature for a variety of valuable purpofes, but principally to promote the happinefs and benefit of man-
kind ; amongft which, the conveyance of the produce of that immenfe and fertile country, lying weftward of the United States, down its ftream to the
Gulf of Mexico, is not the leaft. To expect the free
navigation of the Miffiffippi is abfurd, whilft the Spaniards are in poffeffion of New Orleans, which commands the entrance to the weftern country abovementioned ; this is an idea calculated to impofe only
upon the weak. The Spaniards have forts on the
Miffiffippi, and whenever they may think it confift-
ent with their intereft, they will make ufe of them to
prevent our navigating on it. Treaties are not always to be depended on ; the moft folemn have been
broken* : therefore we learn that no one fhould put
much faith in the princes of any country : for he that
trufts to any thing but the operation of their intereft,
is a poor politician ; and he that complains of deceit,
where there is an intereft to deceive, will ever be confidered as deficient in underftanding.

The great length and uncommon depth of that
river,

* Notwithftanding the free navigation of the Miffiffippi allowed by the treaty of 1762, General O'Riley, in the year 1769, fent a party of foldiers to cut the hawfers of a Britifh veffel called the Sea Flower, that had made faft to the bank of the river above the town of New Or-leans ; the order was obeyed, and the veffel narrowly efcaped being loft.

river, and the exceffive muddinefs and falubrious quality of its waters, after its junction with the Mef-fouri, are very fingular*. The direction of the channel is fo crooked, that from New Orleans to the mouth of the Ohio, a diftance which does not exceed 460 miles in a ftraight line, is about 856 by water. It may be fhortened at leaft 250 miles, by cutting acrofs eight or ten necks of land, fome of which are not 30 yards wide. Charlevoix relates that in the year 1722, at Point Coupeé or Cut Point, the river made a great turn, and fome Canadians, by deepening the channel of a fmall brook, diverted the waters of the river into it. The impetuofity of the ftream was fo violent and the foil of fo rich and loofe a quality that, in a fhort time, the point was entirely cut through, and travellers faved 14 leagues of their voyage. The old bed has no water in it, the times of the periodical overflowings only excepted. ·The new channel has been fince founded with a line of thirty fathoms, without finding bottom.

In the fpring floods the Miffiffippi is very high, and the current fo ftrong that with difficulty it can be afcended; but that difadvantage is compenfated by eddies or counter-currents, which always run in the bends clofe to the banks of the river with nearly equal velocity againft the ftream, and affift the afcending boats. The current at this feafon defcends at the rate of about five miles an hour. In autumn, when the waters are low, it does not run fafter than two miles, but it is rapid in fuch parts of the river, which have clufters of iflands, fhoals and fand-banks. The circumference of many of thefe fhoals being feveral

---

* In a half pint tumbler of this water has been found a fediment of two inches of flime. It is, notwithftanding, extremely wholefome and well tafted, and very cool in the hotteft feafons of the year; the rowers who are then employed drink of it when they are in the ftrongeft perfpiration, and never receive any bad effects from it. The inhabitants of New Orleans ufe no other water than that of the river, which by keeping in jars becomes perfectly clear.

veral miles, the voyage is longer and in fome parts more dangerous than in the fpring. The merchandize neceffary for the commerce of the upper fettlements on or near the Miffiffippi, is conveyed in the fpring and autumn in batteaux rowed by 18 or 20 men, and carrying about 40 tons. From New Orleans to the Illinois, the voyage is commonly performed in eight or ten weeks. A prodigious number of iflands, fome of which are of great extent, interfperfe that mighty river. Its depth increafes as you afcend it. Its waters, after overflowing its banks below the river Ibberville, never return within them again. Thefe fingularities diftinguifh it from every other known river in the world. Below New Orleans the land begins to be very low on both fides of the river acrofs the country, and gradually declines as it approaches nearer to the fea. This point of land which in the treaty of peace in 1762, is miftaken for an ifland, is to all appearance of no long date; for in digging ever fo little below the furface, you find water and great quantities of trees. The many beaches and breakers, as well as inlets, which arofe out of the channel within the laft half century, at the feveral mouths of the river, are convincing proofs that this peninfula was wholly formed in the fame manner. And it is certain that when La Salle failed down the Miffiffippi to the fea, the opening of that river was very different from what it is at prefent.

The nearer you approach to the fea, this truth becomes more ftriking. The bars that crofs moft of thefe fmall channels, opened by the current, have been multiplied by means of the trees carried down with the ftreams; one of which ftopped by its roots or branches, in a fhallow part, is fufficient to obftruct the paffage of thoufands more, and to fix them at the fame place. Such collections of trees are daily feen between the Balize and the Miffouri, which fingly

D   would

would supply the largeft city in Europe, with fuel for feveral years. No human force being fufficient for removing them, the mud carried down by the river ferves to bind and cement them together. They are gradually covered, and every inundation not only extends their length and breadth, but adds another layer to their height. In lefs than ten years time, canes and fhrubs grow on them, and form points and iflands, which forcibly fhift the bed of the river.

Nothing can be afferted, with certainty, refpecting its length. Its fource is not known, but fuppofed to be upwards of 3000 miles from the fea as the river runs. We only know that, from St. Anthony's falls, it glides with a pleafant clear ftream, and becomes comparatively narrow before its junction with the Miffouri, the muddy waters of which immediately difcolour the lower part of the river to the fea. Its rapidity, breadth, and other peculiarities then begin to give it the majeftic appearance of the Miffouri which affords a more extenfive navigation, and is a longer, broader and deeper river than the Miffiffippi. It has been afcended by French traders about twelve or thirteen hundred miles, and from the depth of water, and breadth of the river at that diftance, it appeared to be navigable many miles further.

From the Miffouri river to nearly oppofite the Ohio, the weftern bank of the Miffiffippi is (fome few places excepted) higher than the eaftern. From Mine au fer to the Ibberville, the eaftern bank is higher than the weftern, on which there is not a fingle difcernable rifing or eminence, the diftance of 750 miles. From the Ibberville to the fea, there are no eminences on either fide, though the eaftern bank appears rather the higher of the two, as far as the Englifh turn. Thence the banks gradually diminifh in height to the mouths of the river, where they are not two or three feet higher than the common furface of the water.

The

The flime which the annual floods of the river Miffiffippi leaves on the furface of the adjacent fhores, may be compared with that of the Nile, which depofits a fimilar manure, and for many centuries paft has infured the fertility of Egypt. When its banks fhall have been cultivated as the excellency of its foil and temperature of the climate deferve, its population will equal that, or any other part of the world. The trade, wealth and power of America will at fome future period, depend and perhaps center upon the Miffiffippi. This alfo refembles the Nile in the number of its mouths, all iffuing into a fea that may be compared to the Mediterranean, which is bounded on the North and South by the two continents of Europe and Africa, as the Mexican bay is by North and South America. The fmaller mouths of this river might be eafily ftopped up, by means of thofe floating trees with which the river during the floods is always covered. The whole force of the channel being united, the only opening then left would probably grow deep as well as the bar. *Comparifon with the Nile.*

Probability of deepening the channel.

To judge of the produce to be expected from the foil of Louifiana, let us turn our eyes to Egypt, Arabia Felix, Perfia, India, China, and Japan, all lying in correfpondent latitudes. Of thefe China alone has a tolerable government; and yet it muft be acknowledged they all are, or have been, famous for their riches and fertility. When our wandering imagination foars to regions of wealth and terreftrial blifs, it delights in refting on thofe countries we have juft mentioned. *Produce of Louifiana.*

Louifiana is agreeably fituated between the extremes of heat and cold. Its climate varies as it extends towards the North. The fouthern parts, lying within the reach of the refrefhing breezes from the fea, are not fcorched like thofe under the fame latitudes in Africa; and its northern regions are colder than thofe *Its pleafant climate.*

thofe of Europe under the fame parallels, with a wholefome ferene air, very fimilar to the South of France and Lifbon. New Orleans, fituated in 30d. 2 m. which nearly anfwers to the northern coafts of Barbary and Egypt, enjoys the fame temperature of climate with Marfeilles. Not quite two degrees higher in the country of the Natchez, the climate is much more uniform and temperate than at New Orleans. And in the country of the Illinois, which lies about 37 degrees, the fummer feafon is nearly the fame as at Paris in France.

Objections to the navigation of the Miffiffippi removed.

An objection has been often made by mifinformed men, otherwife of great abilities, who too creduloufly believed that the navigation of the Miffiffippi river, on account of its rapid current, was more difficult than it is in reality. It appears from the calculation made by feveral fkilful and experienced travellers, that in the autumn when the waters are low, the current defcends at the rate of about one and a half or two miles in an hour ; and that the waters are in this ftate more than one half of the year. In the fpring when the frefhes are up, or at their greateft height, the current runs at the rate of five or fix miles. It is true that the navigation would be difficult at that feafon, to thofe who fail or row up againft the ftream; but there is no example of fuch folly. When the waters of this river are high, the commodities and produce of the interior country are gathered and prepared for exportation with the defcending current. And when the waters are low, the produce of the interior country is growing to maturity. This is the time for the navigator's importation. Great advantages are likewife taken then from eddy currents. At prefent there are few builders fkilful enough to conftruct veffels better calculated for that navigation, than thofe already mentioned. Time and experience will doubtlefs produce improvements, and render the navigation

vigation of this river nearly as cheap as any other.
But that the Miffiffippi can anfwer every purpofe of
trade and commerce, is proved to a demonftration, *Its advantages for trade and commerce.*
by the rapid progrefs the French, German, and Aca-
dian inhabitants on that river, have made. They
have attained a ftate of opulence never before fo foon
acquired in any new country. And this was effect-
ed under all the difcouragements of an indolent and
rapacious government. It may be further afferted,
that no country in North-America, or perhaps in the *Equal to any country in North-America.*
univerfe, exceeds the neighbourhood of the Miffiffippi
in fertility of foil and temperature of climate. Both
fides of this river are truly remarkable for the very
great diverfity and luxuriancy of their productions.
They might probably be brought, from the favoura-
blenefs of the climate, to produce two annual crops
of Indian corn as well as rice, and with little cultivation would furnifh grain of every kind in the greateft
abundance. But this value is not confined to the fertility and immenfity of champaign lands ; their timber is as fine as any in the world, and the quantities
of live and other oak, afh, mulberry, walnut, cherry,
cyprefs, and cedar, are aftonifhing. The neighbourhood of the Miffiffippi, befides, furnifhes the richeft
fruits in great variety, particularly grapes, oranges,
and lemons in the higheft perfection. It produces
filk, cotton, faffafrafs, faffron and rhubarb; is pecu-
liarly adapted for hemp and flax, and in goodnefs
of tobacco equals the Brazils ; and indigo is at this
prefent a ftaple commodity, which commonly yields
the planter from three to four cuttings. In a word,
whatever is rich or rare in the moft defirable climates
in Europe, feems natural to fuch a degree on the
Miffiffippi ; that France, though fhe fent few or no
emigrants into Louifiana but decayed foldiers, or perfons in indigent circumftances, (and thefe very poor-
ly fupplied with the implements of hufbandry) foon
began

began to dread a rival in her colony, particularly in the cultivation of vines, from which she prohibited the colonists under a very heavy penalty; yet soil and situation triumphed over all political restraints, and the adventurers, at the end of the war in 1762, were very little inferior to the most ancient settlements of America in all the modern refinements of luxury.

Soil and situation triumph over political restraints.

River Missississippi furnishes fish.

The Missississippi furnishes in great plenty several sorts of fish, particularly perch, pike, sturgeon, eel, and calts of a monstrous size. Craw-fish abound in this country; they are in every part of the earth, and when the inhabitants chuse a dish of them, they send to their gardens where they have a small pond dug for that purpose, and are sure of getting as many as they have occasion for. A dish of shrimps is as easily procured : by hanging a small canvas bag with a bit of meat in it to the bank of the river, and letting it drop a little below the surface of the water, in a few hours a sufficient quantity will have got into the bag. Shrimps are found in the Missississippi as far as the Natchez, 348 miles from the sea.

Description of the coast and islands about the mouths of the Missississippi.

Having glanced at the many advantages that will result from the cultivation and improvement of the lands in the neighbourhood of the Missississippi, we now proceed with a description of the coasts and islands about the mouths of that river with directions to mariners.

The coast here is very low and marshy, and it would be difficult to find the entrances of that river, were it not for the houses at the old and new Balize, and the flag staff at the former, which appear some distance at sea. The white clayey colour of the river water remaining unmixed on the surface, is another indication that the Missississippi is not far distant; and though it may be alarming to strangers, as it was to myself when I first beheld it, as it has the appearance of a shoal, yet the foundings are much deeper off the Missississippi than any where else on the coast.　　　It

It is an obfervation faid to be founded one xperience, that where the water of the Mifliflippi incorporates with, and apparently lofes itfelf in the bay of Mexico, the current divides, and generally fets north-eafterly and fouth-wefterly, but out of foundings the currents are in a great meafure governed by the winds; and if they are not attended to, veffels may be driven fouth-weftward beyond the Balize into the bay of St. Bernard, which is reported to be full of fhoals, and confequently a very dangerous navigation.

To come to an anchor off the Balize, veffels ap- *Directions to Mariners.* proaching the land ought to bring the old Balize to bear about W by S, and the new Balize nearly W N W; they will then be about two miles diftant from, and oppofite to the Eaft pafs, or mouth, in 13 or 14 fathom wather : and the ftrong N E and S E winds always occafion great fwells off the Balize, yet when anchored as above directed they may ride in fafety; except a S E wind, which is the moft dangerous, as it blows directly on fhore, fhould come on fo violent as to part them from their anchors, and prevent their carrying fail; in which cafe, if care has not been taken to obtain a good offing, they will drift either on the mud banks into the pafs ala Loutre, which has only eight feet water, or into the bay Briton, where they will be in a critical fituation, on account of the fhoal water for which that bay is remarkable.

The beft precaution againft the confequences of a *Precautions.* fouth-eaft wind will be to get under way before the ftrength of the gale comes on, and to fteer about N by W half W for the ifland called Grand Gofier diftant 7 leagues. In failing round the fouth weftermoft part of which, care fhould be taken to fteer clear of a fhoal that runs out from it W S W about two miles, which being paffed, veffels fhould luff up, until the S W end of the ifland bears nearly S E two miles ;
there

there is then good anchoring in three and an half fathoms soft bottom.

There is another safe anchoring place in 2 fathom water, just within the S W point of the Isle au Briton; from the S W end of which a shoal runs out nearly half a mile. This island is about a league to the west-ward of the Grand Gosier, and there is good anchoring between them in 3 and 4 fathoms.

If a south-east gale should happen at night, it would be impossible to see the way between the above islands. In that case, a N N E course from the mouths of the Mississippi will clear the chandelures, situated about 3 leagues to the north-ward of the Isle au Grand Gosier, which are better than 9 leagues in length. As all the above islands are low and have no trees growing on them, they cannot be seen at any distance. On that account it will be necessary when sailing towards them, to keep a good look out. There is drift wood on these islands, and fresh water may be got by digging. The water between the chandelures and the peninsula of Orleans is full of shoals, and the navigation fit only for small craft.

Months of the Mississippi how formed. The river Mississippi discharges itself into the gulph of Mexico by several mouths of different depths of water: in the year 1772, that called the south-east in latitude 29 d 10 m North, and longitude 89 d 10 m West from London afforded 12 feet; the East mouth, which before the above period furnished 15 feet, had then no more than 10 and an half feet; and the north-east only 9 and an half feet on the bar of it. The latter now affords 12 feet, and S W has sixteen feet. The bars are subject to shift; but immediately after entering the river, there is from 3 to 7, 8 and 10 fathoms as far as the south-west pass, and from thence 12, 15, 20 and 30 fathoms is the general depth for 1142 computed miles to the Missouri river.

The

The fhoals about the Miffiflippi are formed from
the trees, mud, leaves, and a variety of other matter
continually brought down by the waters of the river,
which being forced along by the current, until repel-
led by the tides, then fubfide, and occaſion what are
commonly called the bars : their diftance from the
entrances of the river, which is generally about 2
miles, depend much on the winds being accidentally
with or againft the tides : when thefe bars accumulate
fufficiently to refift the tides and the current of the
river, they form numerous fmall iflands, which by
conftantly increafing, join to each other and at laft
reach the continent.

All the land bordering the mouths of the Miffiffippi has been made in this manner. It is more than
probable that the whole of the country on both fides
of the river as far as the Ibberville, a diftance of 204
miles, has been produced in a fucceffion of ages by the
vaft quantities of mud, trees, leaves &c. brought
down by the annual floods which overflow the banks
of the Miffiffippi ; the large trunks or bodies of trees
which have been frequently found in digging in the
above diftance, feems to confirm this opinion ; and it
may reafonably be fuppofed, that the lakes on each
fide of this river are parts of the fea not yet filled up:
thus the land is annually raifed and conftantly gains on
the fea. The old Balize, a fmall port erected by the
French on a little ifland, was in the year 1734, at
the mouth of the river, it is now two miles above it.
In the year 1766, Don Antonio D'Ulloa erected
fome barracks on a fmall ifland, the new Balize, (to
which he gave the name of St. Carlos) for the conve-
nience of pilots, and other purpofes, being near the
fouth-eaft entrance of the river, and a more dry and
higher fituation than any there abouts. There was
not the leaft appearance of this ifland 30 years ago*.

E The

---

* Whatever doubts may arife refpecting the above account, there are
not

The old and new Balize were formerly very inconfiderable pofts, with 3 or 4 cannon in each, and garrifoned by a fubaltern's command. Such are their fituations that they neither defend the Miffiffippi, nor the deepeft channel into it, and appear to have been eftablifhed only for the purpofes of affifting veffels coming into the river, and forwarding intelligence or difpatches to New Orleans.

In afcending the Miffiffippi there are extenfive natural meadows, with a profpect of the fea, on both fides, moft part of the diftance to the Detour aux Plaquemines, which is 32 miles : from thence to the fettlements 20 miles further, the whole is a continued tract of low and marfhy grounds, generally overflowed, and covered with thick wood, Palmetto bufhes, &c. which appear almoft impenetrable to either man or beaft. From thence the banks of the river

are well inhabited to the Detour des Anglois, where
the

---

not inftances wanting to prove that fome other parts of the earth have been formed in a fimilar manner, as will appear by the following facts.

Havre de Grace is fituated in the Pays de Caux, about 18 leagues from Rouen, and as much from Dieppe, on the point of a large valley at the mouth of the river Seine, in the latitude of 49 degrees 30 minutes North. It ftands upon a plain fpot of ground, full of moraffes, and croffed by a great number of creeks, and ditches full of water, which contribute not a little to its fecurity. This ground was originally gained out of the fea, and formed from the large quantities of fand, gravel, and mud, which the force of the tide and the river conveyed to that place in a long courfe of time and by infenfible degrees. And as it was formed, fo it feems to be daily increafed by the fame means : for we are affured by a late author*, that about 70 or 80 years ago, the fea, at high water, came very near that gate of the city which is next the harbour; whereas now the high water mark is nearly half a mile diftant from it. So that it appears, the fea has gradually given way, and, as it were, retired to leave the earth at liberty to enlarge and extend itfelf. Nor onght we to be furprifed at this. The ground on which the city of Tyre is built, though now united to the continent, being formerly part of an ifland. Venice would have had the fame fate long ago, had it not been for the great pains the inhabitants have taken to prevent it: the fea formerly wafhed the walls of Ravenna, which is now a league diftant from it; nor are other inftances of this kind wanting, even in the fame kingdom of France, particularly Frejus and Narbonne, a few centuries ago, were on the fhore of the Mediterranean ; but now the one is a league, and the other almoft two, diftant from it.——Defcription de la Haute Normandie, tom. i. p. 193.

* Piganiol de la Force, Nouvelle defcription de la France, tom. ix. page 593.

the circular direction of the river is fo very confiderable that veffels cannot pafs it with the fame wind
that conducted them to it, and muft either wait for a
favourable wind, or make faft to the bank, and haul
clofe, there being fufficient depth of water for any
veffel that can enter the river. The two forts and
batteries at this place, one of each, on both fides of
the river, are more than fufficient to ftop the progrefs
of any veffel whatever*. The diftance from hence to
New Orleans is 18 miles. The Banks of the river
are fettled and well cultivated, and there is a good
road for carriages all the way.

Nothing with certainty can be determined refpecting the time a veffel may take in failing from the Balize to New Orleans, a diftance of 105 miles. With
favourable winds the voyage has been performed in
3 or 4, but it generally takes 7 or 8 days, and fometimes two or three weeks. There is always fhoal
water near the low points of land covered with wil-
lows. In approaching them, a few cafts of the lead
will be neceffary; and in feveral places there are trees
fixed with one end in the bottom, and the other juft
below the furface of the river, and in the fame direction with the current, which by continual friction
of the water, are reduced to a point; and as there
are inftances of veffels failing with force againft them
being run through their bottoms, and finking immediately after, too much care cannot be taken to avoid
them. Attention fhould alfo be paid to keep clear of
the trees floating down the river during the floods†.

The

---

* Doctor Cox of New Jerfey afcended the Miffiffippi to this place in
the year 1698, took poffeffion, and called the country Carolina.

† It is impofible to anchor without being expofed to the danger of
the great trees, which frequently come down with the current, but
more efpecially at the time of the floods, which if any of them fhould
come athwart hawfe, would moft probably drive in the bows of the veffel;
and

The water is every where deep enough (except at the Willow Points) to admit vessels close to either shore, where instead of letting go an anchor, which would probably be lost among the logs sunk in the bottom of the river, vessels may safely make fast to the trees on the bank; which are generally tall and in such abundance, in some parts, that they prevent the winds from being of that service to vessels in ascending the Mississippi, that might be expected. It will be therefore necessary for expedition sake, to rigg as many topsails as possible, which commonly reach above ' the trees and are of more use than all the other sails together; however, care must be taken to stand by the halliards to prevent the wind, which frequently comes in very strong puffs, from carrying away the top-masts, sails, &c.

Town and fortifications of New Orleans.

The town of New Orleans, the metropolis of Louisiana, was regularly laid out by the French in the year 1720, is situated on the East side of the river in 30 d 2 m North latitude, 105 miles from the Balize, as already mentioned; all the streets are perfectly straight but too narrow, and cross each other at right angles. There are betwixt seven and eight hundred houses in this town, generally built with timber frames raised about eight feet from the ground, with large galleries round them, and the cellars under the floors level with the ground: any subteraneous buildings would be constantly full of water. Most of the houses, have gardens. Exclusive of slaves, there are about seven thousand inhabitants of both sexes. The fortification is only a line of stockades, with bastions of the

and there is a certainty of losing the anchors, as the bottom of the river is very soft mud, covered with sunk logs. this points out the impossibility for vessels to navigate upon the Mississippi, unless they are permitted to make fast to the shore ; and no vessel can be said to enjoy the free navigation of the river, if deprived of this necessary privilege.

the fame materials, on three fides, a banquet within, and a very trifling ditch without, and is only a defence against mufquetry. The fide next the river is open, and is fecured from the inundation of the river by a raifed bank, generally called the Leveé, which extends from the Englifh Turn, or the Detour des Anglois, to the upper fettlements of the Germans, a diftance of more than 50 miles, with a good road all the way. There is reafon to believe the period is not very diftant when New Orleans may become a great and opulent city, if we confider the advantages of its fituation, but a few leagues from the fea, on a noble river, in a moft fertile country, under a moft delightful and wholefome climate, within two weeks fail of Mexico by fea, and ftill nearer the French Spanifh and Britifh iflands in the Weft Indies, with a moral certainty of its becoming a general receptacle for the produce of that extenfive and valuable country on the Miffiffippi, Ohio, and its other branches; all which are much more than fufficient to enfure the future wealth, power and profperity of this city.

It may become a great and opulent city.

The veffels which fail up the Miffiffippi haul clofe along fide the bank next to Orleans, to which they make faft, and take in or difcharge their cargoes with the fame eafe as from a wharf.

Eafy loading and unloading veffels.

From New Orleans there is a very eafy communication with Weft-Florida, by means of the Bayouk of St. John, a little creek which is navigable for veffels drawing about four feet water fix miles up from the lake Ponchartrain, where there is a landing-place, at which veffels load and unload : this is about two miles from the town. The entrance of the Bayouk of St. John is defended by a battery of five or fix cannon. There are fome plantations on the Bayouk, and on the road from thence to New Orleans.

Canes-Brulé, Chapitoula, and the German fettlements join each other, and are a continuation of well-

Canes-Brulé, Chapitoula, and the German fettlements.

well-cultivated plantations, of near fifty miles from New Orleans, on each side of the river. At the German settlements, on the West side of the river, is a church served by the Capuchins. There was formerly a small stockaded fort in the centre of the settlements on the East side of the river: this post was originally erected as an asylum for the inhabitants who first settled there, and were much molested by the Chactaws and Chickasaws, who in alliance carried on a war against the settlers on the Mississippi. Their entry into this part of the colony was very easy, as they went up a small creek, Tigahoe, in canoes. The entrance of this creek, which is in the lake Pontchartrain, was defended by a small redoubt, since in ruins.

Produce of the plantations, &c. The produce of the plantations, commencing below the English Turn, and continuing to the upper settlements of the Germans, form a very considerable part of the commerce of this country; the different articles are indigo, cotton, rice, beans, myrtle-wax and lumber. The indigo is much esteemed for its beautiful colour and good quality; the colour is brighter than that which is fabricated at St. Domingo. The cotton formerly cultivated, though of a most perfect white, is of a very short staple, and is therefore not in great request. The different sorts of beans, rice, and myrtle candles, are articles in constant demand at St. Domingo.

Sugar made with success. In the year 1762, several of the richest planters begun the cultivation of sugar, and erected mills to press the canes; the sugar produced was of a very fine quality, and some of the crops were very large: but no dependance can be had on this article, as some years the winters are too cold, and kill the canes in the ground.

Slaves how employed in autumn. In the autumn, the planters employ their slaves in cutting down and squaring timber, for sawing into

boards

boards and scantling. The carriage of this timber is very easy, for those who cut it at the back of their plantations make a ditch, which is supplied with water from the back swamps, and by that means conduct their timber to the river with very little labour: others send their slaves up to the cypress swamps, of which there are a great many between New Orleans and Point Coupée. There they make rafts of the timber they cut, and float down to New Orleans. Many of the planters have saw-mills, which are worked by the waters of the Mississippi, in the time of the floods, and then they are kept going night and day till the waters fall. The quantity of lumber sent from the Mississippi to the West India islands is prodigious, and it generally goes to a good market.

About 60 miles from New Orleans are the villages Villages of the Humas and Alibamas. of the Humas and Alibamas. The former were once a considerable nation of Indians, but are reduced now to about 25 warriors; the latter consists of about 30, being part of a nation which lived near fort Touloufe, on the river Alibama, and followed the French when they abandoned that post in the year 1762. Three miles further up is the Fourche de Fourche de Chetimachas. Chetimachas, near which is the village of a tribe of Indians of the same name; they reckon about 27 warriors.

It is truly surprising, that the nations who have successively possessed Louisiana, never endeavoured to obtain an exact knowledge of the sea coast westward of the mouths of the Mississippi. The many difficulties and dangers to which vessels are exposed in making, and getting over the shallow and shifting bars of that river, as well as in a long and tedious navigation upwards of thirty leagues to New Orleans, would render a harbour to the westward of the Balize, and a water communication with the upper parts of the Mississippi of vast importance. The nature of the narrow

row flip of land extending upwards of 60 leagues be-tween that river and the fea, in a wefterly courfe, indi-cates very ftrongly the probability of a better and more eafy communication from that quarter, than that by the river Ibberville through the lakes Ponchartrain and Maurepas. This opinion is fully confirmed by the information received from Natchiabe, an intelli-gent chief of the Humas tribe, who inhabit the banks of a creek known by the name of the Chetimachas fork, already mentioned, and which I am now to def-cribe. The Chetimachas forms one of the outlets of the Miffiffippi about 30 leagues above New Orleans, and after running in a foutherly direction about 8 leagues from the river, divides into two branches, one of which runs fouth-wefterly and the other fouth-eafterly, to the diftance of 7 leagues, when they both empty their waters into the Mexican Gulph.

On the Chetimachas, 6 leagues from the Miffiffippi, is a fmall fettlement of a tribe of Indians of the fame name. To this fettlement the Chetimachas is uni-formly about 100 yards in width, the depth from 2 to 4 fathoms, when the water is loweft. The courfe foutherly, without any material winding or fhoal, except at its rife from the Miffiffippi, where there are large collections of drifted logs, which have probably occafioned the fand bank formed at the fame place. This bank however extends no farther than 60 yards, and through which a paffage might eafily be cleared for batteaux. The upper part of this outlet is alfo obftructed, in feveral places, by heaps of drifted logs fimilar to thofe juft mentioned, but as the water, at all times, runs deep under them, they could eafily be cleared off. It would be as eafy to prevent any fur-ther collection of logs, or fands, at the entrance of this creek, by erecting a fpar, with piles or caffoons, a little above it, in an oblique direction with the cur-rent of the Miffiffippi. That difficulty once overcome,

there

there is no other that can impede navigation from the river to the above mentioned fettlement of the Chetimachas village; nor, as thefe Indians inform, to the Gulph. The banks on both fides of the Chetimachas, are generally higher than thofe of the Miffiffippi, and fo elevated in fome places as never to be overflowed. The ground rifes gradually from its banks about 200 yards, and then gently defcends to extenfive cyprefs fwamps. The natural productions are the fame as on the Miffiffippi, but the foil from the extraordinary fize and compactnefs of the canes growing on it, is fomething fuperior. If meafures were adopted and purfued with a view to improve that communication, there would foon be, on its banks, the moft profperous and important fettlements of that colony.

Nine miles above the Chetimachas is the *conceffion* of Monfieur Paris, a pleafant fituation and good land. Large herds of cattle are generally kept here, belonging to the inhabitants of Point Coupée.

The fettlements of the Acadians are on both fides The fettlements of Acadians. of the river, and reach from the Germans to the Iberville. Thefe are the remainder of the families which were fent by Gen. Lawrance from Nova Scotia to the then Britifh fouthern provinces; where, by their induftry, they did and might have continued to live very happy, but that they could not publicly enjoy the Roman catholic religion, to which they are greatly bigotted. They took the earlieft opportunity, after the peace, of tranfporting themfelves to St. Domingo, where the climate difagreed with them fo much, that they, in a few months, loft near half their numbers; the remainder, few only excepted, were, in the latter end of the year 1763, removed to New Orleans at the expence of the king of France. There are about three hundred families of this unfortunate people fettled in different parts of Louifiana. They

F   are

are sober and industrious; they clothe themselves in almost every respect with the produce of their own fields, and the work of their own hands, and are very obedient and useful subjects.

The river Ibberville is 99 miles from New Orleans, 204 miles from the Balize, and 270 miles from Penfacola, by the way of the lakes Ponchartrain and Maurepas.

In 1765 a post was established here, and the garrison, which was a detachment of the 34th regiment, withdrawn in the month of July in the same year. In December 1766, this post was re-possessed, and a small stockaded fort built by a party of the 21st regiment, and was demolished and abandoned in 1768. And in the year 1778 it was again possessed by part of the 16th regiment, who were made prisoners by the Spaniards in the year following.

Before the cession of Louisiana to Spain, the peltries of the British and French shores of the Illinois have been mostly carried in the British dominions, either in Canada, by the upper parts of the Mississippi through Machillimakinak, or by the way of New Orleans at the mouth of that river. Philadelphia and New-York have also received great quantities of peltries in return for their flour and the dry goods which they have sent to New Orleans, for the Indian trade, or the use of the inhabitants. Penfacola received likewise large parcels of skins and furs, which have been exported thence to London, to South-Carolina, or other parts of America. This is the reason why the importance of the Illinois or upper Mississippi has, till now, been little known. It is even certain, that it has been artfully concealed by many, who availed themselves of the ignorance of the public on that head.

This would not have been the case, had not the British government withdrawn in 1768, the garrison of fort Bute, which was constructed at Manchac, on the

the bank of the Miffiffippi, oppofite to another fort which the French erected in 1767, at the diftance of about 400 paces from the Britifh fort. Thefe forts were fituated near the place which, in the treaty of peace in 1762, is defcribed as the mouth of Ibberville river to the North of New Orleans ifland, and the then boundary-line of the poffeffions of the two crowns in thofe parts; but the plenipotentiaries of the two powers were mifinformed; for, as we have already obferved, the city of New Orleans is not in an ifland, but on the continent. Or if the tract of land on which that city is fituated, can be termed an ifland, that name can with propriety be applied to it during only two, or at moft three months every year, when the Miffiffippi overflows; an accidental communication with lake Ponchartrain is then opened through the Gut of Ibberville. It may be dignified, during that fhort period, with the title of river, but dries up as foon as the Miffiffippi ceafes to overflow. At any other time the walking from Englifh to French, now Spanifh Manchac, is perfectly dry.

This place, if attended to, might be of confequence to the commerce of Weft-Florida; for it may with reafon be fuppofed, that the inhabitants and traders who refide at Point Coupeé, at Natchitoches, Attacappa, the Natchez, on the Eaft fide of the Miffiffippi above and below the Natchez, at the Illinois, and St. Vincents on the Ouabafhe, would rather trade at this place than at New Orleans, if they could have as good returns for their peltry and the produce of their country; for it makes a difference of ten days in their voyage, which is no inconfiderable faving of labour, money, and time. The only difficulty which oppofes itfelf to this neceffary eftablifhment, is the want of a navigation through the river Ibberville, fo that veffels might carry on a conftant intercourfe betwixt this place and Penfacola without going up the Miffiffippi,

fippi, which is a more tedious navigation. However, this difficulty is greatly obviated by a good road made for carriages between the navigable water of the Ibberville (a diftance of ten miles) and the Miffiffippi ; and when the latter is high enough to run into the former, which it generally is during the months of May, June, and July, veffels drawing from three to four feet, or more, may then pafs from one to the other.

Village of Alibama Indians. About a mile above the Ibberville, on the Eaft fide of the Miffiffippi, there is a village of Alibama Indians, confifting of twenty-five warriors.

Point Coupeè fettlement. From the Ibberville to the fettlements of Point Coupeé is 35 miles; they extend full 20 miles on the Weft fide of the Miffiffippi, and there are fome plantations back on the fide of what is generally called La Faufe Riviere, through which the Miffiffippi paffed about 70 years ago, making the fhape of a crefcent. The fort, which is a fquare figure with four baftions, built with ftockades, is fituated on the fame fide of the Miffiffippi, about four and a half miles above the loweft plantation. The inhabitants of Point Coupeé amount to about 2000 of all ages and fexes, and 7000 flaves. They cultivate tobacco, indigo, and Indian corn ; raife vaft quantities of poultry, which they fend to market at New Orleans, and furnifh to the fhipping. They fquare a great deal of timber and make ftaves, which they convey in rafts to New Orleans. Eight miles above the fort at Point Coupeé, on the fame fide of the river, is a fmall village of the **Affagoula Indians.** Affagoula Indians. They have only about a dozen warriors.

Village of Tonicas. On the Eaft fide of the river, and oppofite to the upper plantations of Point Coupeé, is the village of the Tonicas, formerly a numerous nation of Indians ; but their conftant intercourfe with the white people, and immoderate ufe of fpirituous liquors, have reduced them to about twenty warriors.

About

About ten miles above the Tonicas village, on the fame fide of the river, is a village of Pafcagoula Indians, of twenty warriors; and a little lower down, on the oppofite fide, there is a village of Biloxi Indians, containing thirty warriors.

The Chafalaya is about 30 miles above the fettle- ment of Point Coupeé, and 3 miles below the mouth of the river Rouge. It is the uppermoft mouth of the Miffiffippi, and after running many miles through one of the moft fertile countries in the world, falls into the Bay of St. Bernard, a confiderable diftance weftward of the mouths of the Miffiffippi.

Fifty-four miles from the Miffiffippi down the Chafalaya, on the eaftern fide, is the place called the Portage, juft above the mouth of a fmall rivulet. This Portage is 18 miles from Point Coupeé. Twelve miles below this Portage is a narrow ifland 24 miles long. The eaftern channel is choaked up with logs, but the weftern affords good navigation. The river Appaloufa communicates with this channel nearly oppofite the middle of the ifland, on the Weft fide. There are two fettlements on the Appaloufa; the firft is 30 miles, and the other 12 miles further, from its mouth. In defcending the Chafalaya it is 3 miles from the laft mentioned ifland to Ifle au Vauche; and to the bay de Chafalaya, which is on the eaftern fide of the river, it is 3 miles more. This bay is of a triangular figure, about 6 miles in length, and fomething better than a mile in width at its entrance. When the Chafalaya is not raifed with frefhes, there is feldom more than 5 feet water in this bay. Fifteen miles from it on the eaftern fide, is the bay of Plaquimenes. About half the diftance between thefe bays, is a rivulet which communicates with the former bed of the Miffiffippi, back of Point Coupeé, during the annual floods in that river. The country between them is very low, fwampy and full of ponds of water.

Near

Near the fource of the Chafalaya the current is very rapid, but gradually diminifhes to the mouth, where it is very gentle.

Ifle au Vauche.

We will now return to the Ifle au Vauche, and proceed from thence to lake de Portage, which is 3 miles from the ifland. This lake is 13 miles long, and not more than one and an half broad. It communicates at the fouthern end, by a ftrait a quarter of a mile wide, with the grand lake of Chetimachas, which is 24 miles in length and 9 in width. The country bordering thefe lakes is low and flat, and timbered principally with cyprefs, fome live and other kinds of oak ; and on the eaftern fide, the land between it and the Chafalaya river, is divided and again fubdivided by innumerable fmall ftreams, which occafion as many iflands. Some of thefe ftreams are navigable.

At a little diftance from the fouth-eaftern fhore of the lake Chetimachas, is an ifland where perfons pafling that way generally halt as a refting place. Nearly oppofite this ifland, along the weftern fhore, there is an opening which leads to the fea. It is about 150 yards wide, and has 16 or 17 fathoms water. From the lake along this opening it is 3 miles to the Tage river, which is on the North fide. Three fmall rivulets fall in on the fame fide, in the above diftance; and 3 miles below the Tage river on the weftern fide is a large favanna known by the name of Prairu de Jacko. From this favanna it is about 33 miles to the fea.

Tage river.

In afcending the Tage river, it is 10 leagues from its mouth to an old Indian village, on the Eaft fide, called Mingo Luoac, which fignifies Fire Chief. From this village to the habitation of Monf. Mafs, which is on the Weft fide, it is 2 leagues. One and an half leagues further up, on the Eaft fide, is the village de Selieu Rouge, from whence there is a portage of half a mile to lake Chetimacha. Two leagues further up the river, and on the Weft fide, is the habitation of Monf.

Monf. Sorrel. From whence, to the town la Nouvelle Iberie, on the fame fide, it is fix leagues. The whole of this diftance is tolerably well fettled. From this town about fix leagues wefterly acrofs the country is fituated the village de Skunnemoke or the Tuckapas, on the Vermillion river, which runs into the bay of St. Bernard. The river Tage, is in general better than 100 yards wide, with a gentle current, and a fmall ebb and flow of about 8 or 10 inches. It narrows as you afcend it, where in fome places, it is not 50 yards over. Veffels drawing from 7 to 8 feet water may go from the fea to this town without any obftructions. About 3 leagues above la Nouvelle Iberie is la Force Point, formerly fettled by French neutrals. It is now inhabited by creoles of the country, Spaniards from the Canarie iflands, and a few Englifh from the eaftern fide of the Miffiflippi. Then to la Shute branch, which paffes over a fall of about 10 feet, near to where it enters into the Tage river, it is 3 leagues, and inhabited the whole diftance. From this branch to Monf. Flemming's is 2 leagues more. A quarter of a mile back from Mr. Flemming's there is lake 3 leagues in circuit. From Mr. Flemming's to the church De fata cappau, which is on the Weft fide of the Tage, it is 1 league further, all which is inhabited. From the church to what is called the bottom of the bite, is two leagues, and the whole diftance clofely fettled. From thence to the point fettlement of Acadians is one league, to the plantation of Monf. l'Deé is alfo a league, and to the point of Monf. Deé it is half a league further. From Monf. Deé's to Monf. Fuzelliere's is 5 leagues by water, but only three by land. Fuzelliere's fork, or branch, is juft below his houfe, and divides the diftricts of Attacappau and Appaloufe. And, at the diftance of about 2 leagues, this branch communicates with the Vermillion river wefterly. The river Tage ftill continues to the eaftward. At one

Church De-fata cappau.

Diftricts of Attacappau and Appaloufe.

and

and an half leagues from the fork, or branch, is the Prairie de Monf. Man, to Monf. Man's plantation it is one and an half leagues further ; from thence upwards the river divides into little brooks, and lofes itfelf in rich and extenfive favannahs.

Inhabitants. All the Indians in this part of the country, confifting of feveral fmall tribes, do not exceed 100 families. The white people are about 400 families, and can raife 500 militia. The number of negroes are nearly equal to the whites.

Soil and Produce. Although this country might produce all the valuable articles raifed in other parts of the globe, fituated in the fame latitudes, yet the inhabitants principally cultivate indigo, rice, tobacco, indian corn and fome wheat ; and they raife large ftocks of black cattle, horfes, mules, hogs, fheep and poultry. The fheep is faid to be the fweeteft mutton in the world. The black cattle, when fat enough for fale, which they commonly are the year round, are driven acrofs the country to New Orleans, where there is always a good market.

This country is principally timbered with all the different kinds of oak, but moftly with live oak of the largeft and beft quality, uncommonly large cyprefs, black walnut, hickory, white afh, cherry, plumb, poplar trees, and grape vines ; here is found alfo a great variety of fhrubs and medicinal roots. The lands bordering the rivers and lakes are generally well wooded, but at a fmall diftance from them are very extenfive natural meadows, or favannas, of the moft luxuriant foil, compofed of a black mould about one and a half feet deep, very loofe and rich, occafioned, in part, by the frequent burning of the favannas ; below the black mould, it is a ftiff clay of different colours. It is faid this clay, after being expofed fometime to the fun, becomes fo hard that it is difficult either to break or bend, but when wet by

a light

a light fhower of rain, it flackens in the fame manner
ns lime does when expofed to moifture, and becomes
loofe and moulders away ; after which it is found excellent for vegetation.

This country being fituated between the latitudes Climate.
of 30 and 31 d. North, the climate is of courfe very
mild and temperate ; white frofts, and fometimes thin
ice have been experienced here; but fnow is very uncommon.

The river Rouge, which is fo called from its wa- River Rouge.
ters being of a reddifh colour, and faid to tinge thofe
of the Miffiffippi at the time of the floods. Its fource
is in New Mexico, and it runs about 600 miles.
The river Noir empties itfelf into this river about 30
miles from its confluence with the Miffiffippi, which
is 187 miles from New Orleans. The famous Ferdinand Soto ended his difcoveries and his life at the
entrance of this river, and was buried there. Near
70 leagues up this river the French had a very confiderable poft, Natchitoches. It was a frontier on the
Spanifh fettlements, being 20 miles from the fort of
Adaies. The French fort was garrifoned by a captain's
command. There were forty families fettled here,
confifting moftly of difcharged foldiers and fome merchants who traded with the Spaniards. A great
quantity of tobacco was cultivated at this poft, and
fold for a good price at New Orleans, being held in
great efteem. They fent alfo fome peltry, which they
received in trade from the neighbouring Indians.

From the river Rouge to fort Rofalie it is fifty-fix Fort Rofalie.
and a quarter miles. This fort is fituated in the
country known by the name of the Natchez, in 31 d.
40 m. North latitude, about 243 computed miles from
New Orleans, and 348 from the Balize, following
the courfe of the river. The foil, at this place, is Soil at the
fuperior to any of the lands on the borders of the ri- Natchez.
ver Miffiffippi, for the production of many articles.

G   Its

Its fituation being higher, affords a greater variety of foil, and is in a more favourable climate for the growth of wheat, rye, barley, oats, &c. than the country lower down, and nearer to the fea. The foil alfo produces, in equal abundance, Indian corn, rice, hemp, flax, indigo, cotton, pot-herbs, pulfe of every kind, and pafturage ; and the tobacco made here is efteemed preferable to any cultivated in other parts of America. Hops grow wild ; all kinds of European fruits arrive to great perfection, and no part of the known world is more favourable for the raifing of every kind of ftock. The climate is healthy and temperate ; the country delightful and well watered ; and the profpect is beautiful and extenfive, variegated by many inequalities and fine meadows, feparated by innumerable copfes, the trees of which are of different kinds, but moftly of walnut and oak. The rifing grounds, which are clothed with grafs and other herbs of the fineft verdure, are properly difpofed for the culture of vines ; the mulberry trees are very numerous, and the winters fufficiently moderate for the breed of filk worms. Clay of different colours, fit for glafs works and pottery, is found here in great abundance ; and alfo a variety of ftately timber fit for houfe and fhip building, &c. The elevated, open, and airy fituation of this country renders it lefs liable to fevers and agues (the only diforders ever known in its neighbourhood) than fome other parts bordering on the Mifliffippi, where the want of fufficient defcent to convey the waters off occafions numbers of ftagnant ponds, whofe exhalations infect the air.

This country was once famous for its inhabitants, who from their great numbers, and the ftate of fociety they lived in, were confidered as the moft civilized Indians on the continent of America. They lived fome years in great friendfhip with the French, whom they permitted to fettle on their lands, and to whom
they

they rendered every fervice in their power. Their hofpitality, it feems, was repaid in fuch a manner, that they determined to get rid of their guefts; for on the eve of St. Andrew 1729, they furprifed the fort, and put the whole garrifon to death. At the fame time they made a maffacre of the inhabitants, in which upwards of 500 were killed; fome of the women and children they made prifoners; and very few of either fex efcaped. The whole colony armed to revenge their flaughtered countrymen, and they had feveral fkirmifhes with the Natchez, in which the fuccefs was various. In 1730, Monfieur De Perrier de Salvert, brother to the governor, arrived from France, with the rank of lieutenant-general in Louifiana, and 500 regular troops, who joined the troops and militia of the colony. This army, amounting to 1500 men, went, under the command of the two brothers, to attack the nation of the Natchez; who, with their chiefs, determined to defend themfelves in a fort they had built near a lake which communicates with the Bayouk Dargent, lying Weft of the Natchez, and North of the river Rouge. They invefted this fort, and the Indians made a very refolute and vigorous fally on them, but were repulfed, after a confiderable lofs on both fides. The French having brought two or three mortars, threw fome fhells into the fort, which making a havoc amongft their women and children, fo terrified the Indians, unufed to this fort of war, that they furrendered at difcretion, and were conducted to New Orleans; except a few who had efcaped to the Chickafaws, with their hunters who were providing provifions for their garrifon. Nothing now remains of this nation but their name, by which their country continues to be called. The diftrict of the Natchez, as well as all along the eaftern bank of the Miffiffippi to the river Ibberville, was fettling very faft by daily emigrations from the northern ftates, but the capture of the Britifh

Maffacre of the French in 1729.

Deftruction of Natchez Indians in 1730.

tifh troops on the Miffiffippi, 1779, put an entire
ftop to it.

Petit Goufre.   From fort Rofalie to the Petit Goufre is thirty-
one and a half miles. There is a firm rock on the
Eaft fide of the Miffiffippi for near a mile, which
feems to be of the nature of limeftone. The land
near the river is much broken and very high, with a
good foil, and feveral plantations on it.

Bayouk Pierre.   From the Petit Goufre to Bayouk Pierre, or Stoney
River, is four miles and a quarter. From the mouth
to what is called the fork of this river, is computed
to be 21 miles. In this diftance there are feveral
quarries of ftone, and the land has a clay foil with
gravel on the furface of the ground. On the North
fide of this river the land, in general, is low and rich ;
that on the South fide is much higher, but broken
into hills and vales ; but here the low lands are not
often overflowed: both fides are fhaded with a variety
of ufeful timber. At the fork the river parts almoft
at right angles, and the lands between, and on each
fide of them, are faid to be clay and marl foil, not fo
uneven as the lands on this river lower down.

Loufa Chitto.   From the Bayouk Pierre to Loufa Chitto, or the
Big Black, at the Grand Goufre, is 10 miles. The Big
Black (or Loufa Chitto) is, at the mouth, about 30
yards wide, but within, from 30 to 50 yards, and is
faid to be navigable for canoes 30 or 40 leagues.
About a mile and a half up this river, the high lands
are clofe on the right and are much broken. A mile
and a half further, the high lands appear again on
the right, where there are feveral fprings of water,
but none as yet has been difcovered on the left. At
about eight miles further, the high lands are near the
river, on the left, and appear to be the fame range
that comes from the Yazou cliffs, which are about
twelve miles up the Yazou river. At fix miles further the high lands are near the river on both fides,
and

and continue for two or three miles, but broken and full of fprings of water. This land on the left was chofen by General Putnam, Captain Enos, Mr. Lyman and other New England adventurers, as a proper place for a town; and, by order of the governor and council of Weft Florida in 1773, it was referved for the capital. The country round is very fit for fettlements. For four or five miles above this place, on both fides of the river, the land is rich, and not fo much drowned, nor fo uneven, as fome parts lower down. About fix miles and a half further, there is a rapid water, ftones and gravel bottom 160 yards in length ; and in one place a firm rock almoft acrofs the river, and as much of it bare, when the water is at a moderate height, as confines the ftream to nearly 20 feet; and the channel is about 4 feet deep.

From the Big Black to the Yazou cliffs is 39 miles and three quarters. From this cliff the high lands ly North eaftward and South fouth eaftward, bearing off from the river, full of cane and rich foil, even on the very higheft ridges. Juft at the South end of the cliffs, the bank is low, where the water of the Miffiffippi, when high, flows back and runs between the bank and high land, which ranges nearly northerly and fouth fouth eafterly to the Loufa Chitto, occafioning much wet ground, cyprefs fwamp and ftagnant ponds.

From the Cliffs, or Aux Cotes, is feven miles and a half to the river Yazou. The mouth of this river is upwards of 100 yards in width, and was found by Mr. Gauld to be in latitude 32 d. 37 m. and by Mr. Purcel in 32 d. 28 m. North. The water of the Miffiffippi, when the river is high, runs up the Yazou feveral miles, and empties itfelf again by a number of channels, which direct their courfe acrofs the country, and fall in above the Walnut hills. The Yazou runs from the north-eaft and glides through a healthy fertile

Yazou cliffs.

Yazou river.

tile

tile and pleafant country, greatly refembling that about the Natchez, particularly, in the luxuriancy and diverfity of its foil, variety of timber, temperature of climate and delightful fituation. It is remarkably well watered by fprings and brooks ; many of the latter afford convenient feats for mills. Further up this river the canes are lefs frequent and fmaller in fize, and at the diftance of 20 miles there are fcarcely any. Here the country is clear of underwood and well watered, and the foil very rich, which continues to the Chactaw and Chickafaw towns. The former is fituated on the eaftern branch of the Yazou, an hundred miles from the mouth of that river, and confifts nearly of 140 warriors: the towns of the latter are about 15 miles Weft of the north-weft branch 150 miles from the Miffiffippi. They can raife upwards of 500 warriors. The above branches unite 50 miles from the Miffiffippi, following the courfe of the river; the navigation to their junction, commonly called the fork, is practicable with very large boats in the fpring feafon, and with fmaller ones a confiderable way further, with the interruption of but one fall, where they are obliged to make a fhort portage, 20 miles up the north-weft branch, and 70 miles from the Miffiffippi. The country in which the Chactaw and Chickafaw towns are fituated, is faid to be as healthy as any part of this continent, the natives fcarcely ever being fick. Such of them as frequent the Miffiffippi, leave its banks as the fummer approaches, left they might partake of the fevers that fometimes vifit the low fwampy lands bordering upon that river. Wheat, it is faid, yields better at the Yazou than at the Natchez, owing probably to its more northern fituation. One very confiderable advantage will attend the fettlers on the river Yazou, which thofe at the Natchez will be deprived of, without going to a great expence; I mean the building with ftone, there being great plenty ty near the Yazou, but none has yet been difcovered nearer to the Natchez than the Petit Goufre, or little Whirlpool, a diftance of 31 miles and a half. Between this place and the Balize there is not a ftone to be feen any where near the river. Though the quantity of good land on the Miffiffippi and its branches, from the bay of Mexico to the river Ohio, a diftance of nearly one thoufand miles, is vaftly great, and the conveniences attending it; fo likewife we may efteem that in the neighbourhood of the Natchez, and of the river Yazou the flower of it all.

About a mile and a half up the Yazou river, on the North fide, there is a large creek, which communicates with the Miffiffippi above the river St. Francis, about 100 leagues higher up, by the courfe of the river. It paffes through feveral lakes by the way. At the diftance of twelve miles from the mouth of the river Yazou, on the South fide, are the Yazou hills. There is a cliff of folid rock at the landing place, on which are a variety of broken pieces of fea fhells, and fome entire. Four miles further up is the place called the Ball Ground, near which a church, fort St. Peter, and a French fettlement formerly ftood. They Deftruction of the French were deftroyed by the Yazou Indians in 1729. That in 1729. nation is now entirely extinct.

From the Yazou to the river Arkanfaw is 158 River Arkan- and a quarter miles. It is fo called from a nation of faw. Indians of the fame name. Its fource is nearly in the latitude of Santa Fé in New Mexico, and it is faid to be navigable for batteaux 750 miles. It runs through an immenfely rich and fertile country. About ten or twelve miles up this river from the Miffiffippi there was formerly a fort, garrifoned generally by a company of Spanifh foldiers, for the purpofe of defending the trade carried on between New Orleans and the feveral villages of St. Genevieve, &c. and particularly for defending the commerce with the Arkanfaw

kanfaw Indians, confifting of about 280 warriors, who are as much attached to the French intereft, as the Chickafaws are to that of the Englifh. No fettlements were made here, except one or two for the immediate accommodation of the garrifon. The inundation of the Miffiffippi, about three years ago, occafioned the evacuation of the above poft, and the eftablifhment of another on the northern bank of the river 36 miles higher up. This poft, confifting of a fubaltern's command, fix pieces of cannon and eight fwivels, was attacked about eighteen months fince by a party of Chickafaws, who killed ten foldiers of the garrifon, and foon after concluded a peace with the Spaniards. There is a hamlet clofe to the fort, inhabited only by merchants and traders. The Arkanfaw river difcharges itfelf into the Miffiffippi by two channels, about 15 miles from each other ; the uppermoft is called Riviere Blanche, from its receiving a river of that name, reported to be navigable 600 miles, and the foil through which it runs equal in quality to any on the Miffiffippi.

River St. Francis. From the Arkanfaw river to the river St. Francis, which is on the Weft fide of the Miffiffippi, is 108 miles. This is a fmall river, and is remarkable for nothing but the general rendezvous of the hunters from New Orleans, who winter there, and collect falt meat, fuet, and bears oil, for the fupply of that city. Formerly the French had a poft at the entrance of this river, for a magazine of ftores and provifions during their wars with the Chickafaws, by whom their Illinois convoys were conftantly attacked and frequently deftroyed.

River Margot From the river St. Francis to the river and hights of Margot, which are on the Eaft fide of the Miffiffippi, is 70 and a half miles. This river is faid to be navigable for batteaux a number of miles. It appears to be a pretty little river. The high ground below

its

its junction with the Missississippi affords a commanding, airy, pleasant and extensive situation for settlements; the soil is remarkably fertile. On this ground just below the mouth of the river, the French built a fort, called Assumption Fort, when at war with the Chickasaws, in the year 1736, but it was demolished in the year following, when a peace with those Indians was concluded.

From the river Margot to the Chickasaw river, Chickasaw which is on the East side of the Missississippi, is 104 and River. a half miles. The lands here are of an excellent quality, and covered with a variety of useful timber, canes, &c. This river may be ascended during high floods upwards of 30 miles with boats of several tons burthen.

From the Chickasaw river to Mine au fer, or the Mine au fer. Iron Mines, on the East side of the Missississippi, is 67 and a quarter miles. Here the land is nearly similar in quality to that bordering the Chickasaw river, interspersed with gradual risings or small eminences. There is a post at this place, near the South boundary of Virginia.

From Mine au fer to the Ohio river, which is the Ohio River. largest eastern branch of the Missississippi, is 15 miles. This river, and its principal branches, as also the settlements in the Illinois country, are delineated in a map, and very particularly described in a pamphlet which I published in London, the 1st of January 1778, and to them the reader is referred.

Having briefly touched upon all the settlements on, and principal branches of the Missississippi, from the sea to the river Ohio; I shall now just mention the bounds of West-Florida.

The province of West-Florida is situated on the Bounds of North side of the Gulph of Mexico, and extends from West-Florida. the river Appalachicola, which is the boundary between it and East-Florida, to the Regolets at the entrance

H

trance into lake Ponchartrain, thence through the lakes Ponchartrain and Maurepas, and along the river Ibberville to the Miffiffippi, thence along the Miffiffippi to the northernmoft part of the 31ft deg. of North latitude, thence by a line drawn due Eaft along the South boundary of the ftate of Georgia to the river Appalachicola, including all the iflands within fix leagues of the coaft, between the Appalachicola and lake Ponchartrain.

General obfervations relating to the coaft of Florida. I now proceed to make fome general obfervations, which may be of fervice in making the land when you arrive on the coaft of Florida. This is diftinguifhable many different ways; as by the latitudes, the trenching and direction of the fhore, and the foundings and quality of the bottom, to each of which particular attention muft be paid.

From cape Blaife in 29 d 41 m North latitude, to the Balize at the mouth of the Miffiffippi, the coaft forms a curve, inclining to the northward, for 28 leagues, as far as the Eaft end of Rofe ifland in 30 d 28 m North; from thence the land gradually declines to the fouthward, as far as Mobille Point in 30 d 17 m North about 30 leagues. Dauphin ifland, and the other iflands, including Ship ifland, ftretch nearly Weft for the fpace of 20 leagues, and from the North end of the Chandeleurs, which lies near 5 leagues to the South-eaft of Ship ifland, the coaft runs chiefly to the fouthward till you arrive at the entrance of the river Miffiffippi.

It is likewife to be obferved, that in feveral places there is double land to be feen over the different bays and lagoons: as at St. Andrew's bay; which may be known by a high white fand hill, near the point of a peninfula, on the left hand going in: at St. Rofe's bay; where there is a remarkable red bluff on the Eaft fide of the entrance juft oppofite to the Eaft end of Rofe ifland ; over the greateft part of which ifland double land may likewife be feen from the

the maft head, and at the bay of Penfacola, the entrance of which is remarkable on account of the red
cliff oppofite to the Weft end of Rofe ifland. There
is a large lagoon, a little more than a league to the
weftward of this cliff, about 3 leagues in length, leaving a narrow peninfula, over which the double land
may eafily be feen, with a high red bank on the North
fide about half way ; this feems to diftinguifh it from
any other part of the coaft. There is a double land
at the entrance of the river Perdido; but it is not
eafily obferved at any confiderable diftance. The
fame may alfo be feen over fome parts of Dauphin
ifland, and thofe to the weftward of it, viz. Maffacre,
Horn and Ship iflands, as well as between them; but
it appears at fo great a diftance, that it cannot be
miftaken for any part of the coaft to the eaftward of
Mobille Point.

The Chandeleurs, which were 5 in number, when The Chande-
deleur iflands.
I vifited them in the year 1772, extend nearly S by
W 9 or 10 leagues. The Ifle aux Grand Gozier lies
about 10 or 11 miles to the fouthward of them, with
breakers all the way between. The Ifle au Briton,
or rather a clufter of iflands of that name, lie about
4 miles to the weftward of the Grand Goziers, or
Great Pelican ifland: both thefe and the Chandeleur
iflands are very low, with fome bufhes: and behind
them, at a confiderable diftance, there is a chain of
low marfhy iflands and lagoons, bordering the peninfula of Orleans.

This is a dangerous part of the coaft to a ftranger, A dangerous
part of the
coaft.
both on account of the lownefs of the land, which
cannot be feen at any diftance, as there are no trees,
and likewife on account of the above mentioned fhoal
between the fouthernmoft of the Chandeleurs, and
the Grand Goziers, from latitude 29d 42m North,
to 29 d 32 m North.

There is however very good fhelter for fhips, within

in the North end of the Chandeleurs, in Naſſau road, which lies 5 leagues to the ſouthward of Ship iſland, and is one of the beſt for large veſſels on the whole coaſt of Florida; not only as it affords good ſhelter from thoſe winds that blow on ſhore, but as it is, by having no bar, of ſo eaſy an acceſs from the ſea. Care muſt however be taken, not to go within three quarters of a mile of the inſide of the iſland, it being ſhoal near that diſtance from the ſhore.

Veſſels may go round the North end of it from the ſea, in 5 and a half and 6 fathoms, at half a mile from the ſhore; and afterwards muſt keep in 4 and a half and 5 fathoms, till the North point bears N N E about 2 miles; when they may come to an anchor in 4 fathoms good holding ground, ſheltered from eaſterly and ſoutherly winds.

It would be neceſſary for veſſels to be well acquainted with this road, as eaſterly winds are frequent on the coaſt of Florida. There is freſh water to be got any where on the Chandeleurs by digging; beſides which it might be met with in a kind of well, at an old hut near the North end. No wood is to be found here but drift wood, of which there is great plenty along ſhore.

Naſſau Road was firſt diſcovered by Dr. Daniel Cox of New Jerſey, about the time of King William the 3d, who gave it the name of Naſſau, in honour of that prince. Doctor Cox had likewiſe given the name of the Myrtle iſlands to thoſe which are ſtill ſo denominated, before the French called them the Chandeleurs; and they were ſo named by both, from the candles made of the myrtle wax with which theſe iſlands abound.

River Ibberville. From the Weſt ſide of the * iſthmus of the peninſula of Orleans to the junction of the Ibberville with
lake

* The river Ibberville was very little known by the Engliſh at the treaty of peace in 1762; for notwithſtanding the crown has expended
ſome

lake Maurepas, it is 60 computed miles, following the courfe of the river, which for the firft 10 miles is not navigable above four months in the year ; but there is at all times from two to fix feet for three miles further, and between two and four fathoms is the depth the remaining part of the way to the lake.

The river Amit falls into the Ibberville on the North fide, about 21 miles from the junction of the Ibberville with the Miffiffippi. The water of the Amit is clear, with a gravelly bottom. It may be afcended with veffels drawing five or fix feet water, about half a dozen miles, and with batteaux 100 miles further. Seventeen miles from the Ibberville this river forks ; the weftern branch, called the Comit, has its fource near the country of the Natchez ; and the eaftern branch, which is the moft confiderable, rifes near the Pearl river : both thefe branches run through a very fertile country, in fome parts hilly, which, as well as the low lands, is covered with canes, oaks, afh, mulberry, hickory, poplar, cedar and cyprefs. The banks in general are high, yet in fome parts they are fubject to be overflowed. There were a number of inhabitants fettled on the Amit and Comit, who had flaves, and who raifed indigo, cotton, rice, hemp, tobacco, and Indian corn, in great abundance, and all excellent in their kind. They had plenty of horfes, cows, hogs, poultry, &c. and the river abounds with a variety of fifh.

From the Amit to lake Maurepas is 39 miles, following the Ibberville. The quality of the land and timber

River Amit.

timber on this river is fimilar to that on the Amit,
with this difference, its banks in general are lower
and the country lefs hilly, and there is a greater proportion of rice land, and alfo cyprefs and live oak ;
the latter is of an extraordinary quality for fhip building. There were feveral inhabitants on this river
who raifed indigo, Indian corn, rice, &c. and were
in a very thriving way.

Lake Maurepas is about 10 miles in length and 7
in width, with 10 or 12 feet water in it. The country round it is low, and covered with cyprefs, live
oak, myrtle, &c. Two creeks fall into this lake ;
one from the North fide, called Nattabanie, the other
from the peninfula of Orleans.

From the Ibberville acrofs the lake, it is 7 miles
to the paffage leading to Ponchartrain. The length
of this paffage is 7 miles, and only 300 yards in width,
which is divided into two branches by an ifland that
extends from Maurepas to about the diftance of a
mile from Ponchartrain. The South channel is the
deepeft and fhorteft.

Lake Ponchartrain. The greateft length of this
lake is about 40 miles, breadth 24 miles, and depth
18 feet. The following creeks fall in on the North
fide, Tangipaho and Le Comble, 4 feet deep ; Che-
functa, 7 ; and Bonfouca, 6 ; and from the peninfula of Orleans, Tigahoc, at the mouth of which was
a fmall poft. The Bayouk of St. John, which alfo
communicates on the fame fide, has been already mentioned. The French inhabitants, who formerly re-
fided on the North fide of this lake, chiefly employed themfelves in making pitch, tar, and turpentine,
and raifing ftock, for which the country is very favourable.

The diftance from lake Ponchartrain through the
Regolets is 10 miles, and between 3 and 400 yards,
broad, and lined with marfhes on each fide.

On

On the South side of the Regolets, and near to the entrance from the sea, there is a large paſſage into the lake Borgne, or Blind lake, and, by some creeks that fall into it, small craft may go as far as the plantations on the Miſſiſſippi ; and there is a paſſage between the lakes Borgne and Ponchartrain : but either by this, or that of the Rigolets, fix, and sometimes seven feet, is the deepeſt water through.

Near the entrance at the Eaſt end of the Regolets, and on the North fide, are the principal mouths of Pearl river, which rifes in the Chactaw nation, and is navigable upwards of 150 miles. There is 7 feet going into it, and deep water afterwards. In the year 1769, there were fome settlements on this river, where they raiſed tobacco, indigo, cotton, rice, Indian corn, and all forts of vegetables. The land produces a variety of timber fit for pipe and hogſhead ſtaves, maſts, yards, and all kinds of plank for ſhip building.

From the Regolets to the bay of St. Louis is about 18 miles. This is a fmall beautiful compact bay with about 7 feet water in it: the land near it is of a light foil, and good for paſture. There were feveral fettlers formerly on it, but in the year 1767, the Chactaw Indians killed their cattle and obliged them to remove.

From this bay to the bay of Biloxi, is 26 miles. Juſt oppofite to Ship iſland, on the main land, is fituated old Biloxi, in a fmall bay of the fame name, behind L'Iſle au Chevereuil, or Buck or Deer iſland. This is the place where the French made their firſt eſtabliſhment in Louiſiana: but they did not continue there long, finding it in every reſpect an improper fituation for the capital. There are ſtill a few inhabitants at Biloxi, fome of whom are the offspring of the original fettlers. Their chief employment is raiſing of cattle and ſtock, and making pitch and tar: but the natives are very troublefome to them.

From

From the Biloxi to the Pafcagouli river is about 13
miles. This river empties itfelf by feveral mouths;
between the eaftermoft and weftermoft of which, there
is a fpace of between 3 and 4 miles, that is nearly
one continued bed of oyfter fhells, with very fhoal
water. The only channel is at the weftermoft entrance, where there are 4 feet. This large river about
20 miles above its entrance is divided into two
branches, which continue their courfe to the fea, generally about 5 or 6 miles afunder. The intermedi-
ate fpace, for feveral miles above its mouth, is nothing
but marfhes interfected by lagoons. · After getting
into either of the branches, there is from 3 to 6 fathoms, and the river is faid to be navigable for more
than 150 miles.

The foil on this river, like all other rivers on the
coaft of Weft Florida, grows better the higher up
you go; but even near the entrance it is far from
being bad. There are fome good plantations on the
Eaft fide, but here, as well as all the way to the weftward, the inhabitants are much molefted by the natives, efpecially by the Chactaws who kill their cattle, &c.

From the Pafcagoula river to the Pafs au Heron at
the bay of Mobille is 18 miles. This pafs has 4 feet
water; and from thence to the point, which is on
the Eaft fide of the bay of Mobille, in latitude 30 d
17 m North, is nearly 6 miles.

Before defcribing this bay, I fhall take notice of
the following iflands fituated along the coaft, between
the bay of St. Louis and the point of Mobille.

Cat ifland lies about 8 miles eaftward of the bay of
St. Louis, and 7 miles from the coaft: it is 6 miles
in length, very narrow, and of an irregular fhape,
with a large fhoal from the Eaft end of it, extending
within two miles of Ship ifland. The foil is poor,
producing nothing but pine, fome live oak and grafs,
and

and its fhore is almoft every where covered, or bordered with an immenfity of fhells.

The marfhy iflands near the peninfula of Orleans, are diftant about 3 miles South of Cat ifland ; and between them there is a channel of 9 feet, which continues to the Regolets through a number of fhoals.

Ship ifland is fituated between 7 and 8 miles Eaft of Cat ifland, and about 10 miles South of the bay of Biloxi. This ifland is 9 miles in length and 2 miles in width where broadeft. It produces pine trees and grafs, and there is a well of tolerable water on it. The weftern part of this ifland is very narrow, and for better than three miles there is not a treé on it. A fhoal runs out due South, about a mile from the Weft end. The channel is better than a mile wide with from 4 to 5 and 6 fathoms, but the bar has only 21 feet. In going over it from the fea the courfe to be fteered is due North, keeping the above fhoal near half a mile to the eaftward, and after fairly paffing the end of the ifland, from the inner part of which lies a fhoal, the courfe proceeds N E until the broadeft part of the point of the ifland bears due South about one mile and a half, where there is between 4 and 5 fathoms. This is a good place to anchor in the fummer time; but is very much expofed in winter, when the northerly winds prevail ; and is a very convenient place for fhipping the produce of the rivers Pearl, Ibberville and Amit, and the lakes Maurepas and Ponchartrain.

From Ship ifland to Horn ifland is between 5 and 6 miles, with a fmall key called Dog ifland between, about two thirds of the way, and with a fhoal all the way from the former to about a quarter of a mile of the latter, where there is a channel of 5 fathoms. The above fhoal extends South of the channel nearly 2 miles, where there is a bar of 15 feet; in croffing of which it behoves the mariner to keep about half a

I
· mile

mile from the shore, and to steer for the end of the island, and on approaching it to give it a birth of about a cables length, to avoid a shoal on the left; after passing of which he ought to keep a little to the westward, on account of a shoal that runs from the inside of the island, then to haul round to the eastward, where there is better than 15 feet water, a little more than a mile from the island.

Its description. Horn island is nearly 17 miles in length, and about half a mile in width. There are more trees on the middle of the island than in any other part of it; and for about 3 miles from the East end there are no trees at all, but there are a number of sandy hillocks.

Round island. Round island lies about 5 miles North from opposite the middle of Horn island, and is well timbered.

Island of Massacre. The island of Massacre is upwards of 2 miles to the eastward of Horn island, from which a shoal extends better than a mile and a half between them, leaving a channel of about 11 feet round the West end of Massacre island; but within the island there is between 3 and 4 fathoms.

Massacre is nearly 9 miles long and very narrow, it is remarkable for a grove of trees in the middle, which is the more particular as there is not a tree any where else on the island.

The distance between Massacre island and the main, is about 10 miles, from 2 to 3 fathoms all the way across; except one large shoal called la Grand Bature, which stretches out from the main land about a league, with 2 or 3 feet water on it, and in some places not so much. Behind it, there is a large bay called L'ance de la Grand Bature, 8 miles East of Pascagoula bluff.

The land here and to the eastward, as far as the bay of Mobille, is swampy towards the sea, with a clay bottom for 2 or 3 miles back; but afterwards it is covered chiefly with pines, live oak and hickory, and the soil is sandy or gravelly for several miles, before

it

it becomes truly fit for culture; notwithstanding which it is good for pasture.

From Massacre to Dauphin island is 5 miles, with a shoal all the way between them. These are supposed formerly to have been but one, which went by the general name of Massacre, so called by Monf. d'Ibberville, from a large heap of human bones found thereon at his first landing; but it was afterwards called Dauphin island, in honor of the Dauphin of France, and to take off the disagreeable idea excited by the other name.

Dauphin island is about 10 miles long, and in the broadest part not quite 2 miles. The West end for between 3 and 4 miles, is a narrow slip of land with some dead trees; the rest is covered with thick pines, which come close to the waters edge on the East side, forming a large bluff. There is the remains of an old French post on the South side of the island; about two miles from that bluff are a few old houses on the North side opposite to it, near which are large hillocks of oyster shells, now covered with dwarf cedar and live oak. There are many such vestiges of the antient inhabitants in several bays and other places on the coast, and as these are always found on high banks, the usual places where the natives encamp, it cannot well be supposed they were left there by the sea, though many are of that opinion.

Gillori island is divided from Dauphin island on the North side by a narrow channel, through which a boat may pass with some difficulty; and between Gillori and the main land, on the West side of Mobille bay, there is a chain of small islands, and oyster shells, through which there is a passage of four feet, called Passe au Heron, where small craft may go from Mobille bay to the westward within the islands. There is likewise a passage for small boats and canoes from the West side of the bay of Mobille, through what the French call Riviere aux Poules, which falls in opposite

Dauphin island.

Gillori island.

posite

posite to the West end of Dauphin island, and cuts off a considerable space of ground.

Great Pelican Island. Just opposite the old fort, on the South side of Dauphin island, distant one mile, lies Great Pelican island, which is about a mile in length, and very narrow. It stretches to the S E in form of a half moon, the concave side being towards the East end of Dauphin island. There are neither trees nor bushes on it, but here and there large tufts of grass like small reeds, on the sandy parts near the sea side.

Hawk's Bay. Hawk's bay is between Pelican and Dauphin islands. There is a broad channel of 11 and 12 feet, afterwards safe anchorage in four fathoms good holding ground, and well sheltered from most winds; on which account it is very convenient for small vessels.

Little Pelican Island. There is a small sand key called Little Pelican island, about a league S E from Great Pelican island, forming a curve to the eastward, and there it meets a large shoal extending from Mobille Point.

Directions for entering Mobille Bay. The deepest water on the bar of Mobille, or rather of Mobille bay, (for there is another bar at the entrance of the river near the town) is only 15 or 16 feet. The mark for going over it in the deepest channel, is to bring Little Pelican island well on with the bluff on the East end of Dauphin island, bearing about N N W 3-4 W, and then to steer in for the key in that direction. The Point of Mobille bears from the bar nearly due North four miles, and the key is more than a mile and a half within it. Both the East and West reefs, as well as the bar itself, are steep towards the sea, there being from three to seven and eight fathoms immediately without; this occasions a constant swell with a heavy sea when it blows from the southward : and therefore in rough weather, it would be imprudent to go over it in a vessel that draws above 10 or 11 feet water. Within the bar it deepens gradually towards Little Pelican island, between

tween which and the East reef, the channel is not more than a quarter of a mile broad, with fix or feven fathoms water. This depth continues all the way round Mobille Point, where is tolerable good anchorage in four or five fathoms, but it is at beft an open road-ftead, the bay being too large to afford much fhelter.

From Mobille Point to the town the diftance is about 11 leagues nearly due North, and the breadth of the bay in general is about three or four leagues. At the lower part of it is a deep bight that runs about fix leagues to the eaftward of the point, having a narrow peninfula between it and the fea. The river Bon Secour falls into the bottom of this bay or bight, and Fifh river with that of La Sant on the North fide of it; on which there are feveral habitations. Directions for entering Mobille Bay.

On the Weft fide of the bay of Mobille there are likewife fome fmall rivers, but none confiderable, befides La Riviere aux Poules, by which there is a fmall inland communication to the weftward, and Dog river, which falls into the bay about nine miles below Mobille. The former has five or fix feet in the entrance, and is navigable for a boat feveral miles back into the country. With regard to the general depth of the water in the bay, there is from two to three fathoms two-thirds of the way from Mobille Point towards the town, and the deepeft water to be depended on in the upper part of the bay is only 10 or 12 feet, and in many places not fo much; but there is no danger, as the bottom is foft mud. Large veffels cannot go within feven miles of the town. La Riviere aux Poules, and Dog River.

Notwithftanding all thefe inconveniencies in point of navigation, Mobille having been the frontiers of the French dominions in Louifiana, always was, and now is a very confiderable place. It has a fmall regular fort, built with brick, and a neat fquare of barracks for the officers and foldiers. The town is Town of Mobille.

pretty

pretty regular of an oblong figure, on the West bank of the river, where it enters the bay.

There is a confiderable Indian trade carried on here. Mobille, when in poffeffion of his Britannic Majefty, fent yearly to London, fkins and furs amounting from 12 to 15,000 pounds fterling : it was then the only ftaple commodity in this part of the province. The Britifh garrifon at Mobille furrendered to the arms of his Catholic Majefty in the year 1780.

The bay of Mobille terminates a little to the northeaftward of the town, in a number of marfhes, and lagoons: which fubject the people to fevers and agues in the hot feafon.

Mobille River. The river of Mobille is divided into two principal branches about 40 miles above the town : one of which is called the Tanfa, falls into the Eaft part of the bay ; the other empties itfelf clofe by the town, where it has a bar of 7 feet ; but there is a branch a little to the eaftward of this, called Spanifh river, where there is a channel of 9 or 10 feet, when the water is high, but this joins Mobille river about two leagues above the town.

Alibama River. Two or three leagues above the Tanfa branch, the Alibama river falls into Mobille river, after running from the N E a courfe of about 130 miles ; that is from Alibama fort, fituated at the confluence of the Couffa, and Talpoufe, both very confiderable rivers ; on which and their branches are the chief fettlements of the upper Creek Indians.

The French fort at Alibama was evacuated 1763, and has not fince been garrifoned. Above the confluence of Alibama and Mobille, the latter is called Tombecbe River. the Tombecbe river, from the fort of Tombecbe fituated on the Weft fide of it, about 96 leagues above the town of Mobille. The fource of this river, is reckoned to be about 40 leagues higher up, in the country

country of the Chickafaws. The fort of Tombecbe was taken poffeffion of by the Englifh, but abandoned again in 1767, by order of the commandant of Penfacola. The river is navigable for floops and fchooners about 35 leagues above the town of Mobille. The banks, where low, are partly overflowed in the rainy feafons, which adds greatly to the foil, and adapts it particularly to the cultivation of rice. The fides of the river are covered in many places with large canes, fo thick that they are almoft impenetrable; there is alfo plenty of remarkable large red and white cedar, cyprefs, elm, afh, hickory and various kinds of oak. Several people have fettled on this river, who find the foil to anfwer beyond expectation.

The lands near the mouth of the Mobille river are generally low: as you proceed upwards, the land grows higher, and may with great propriety be divided into three ftages. Firft, low rice lands on or near the banks of the river, of a moft excellent quality. Secondly, what are called by the people of the country fecond low grounds, or level flat cane lands about 4 or 5 feet higher than the low rice lands. And, thirdly the high upland or open country. The firft or low lands extend about an half or 3 quarters of a mile from the river, and may almoft every where be eafily drained and turned into moft excellent rice fields, and are capable of being laid under water at almoft all feafons of the year. They are a deep black mud or flime, which have in a fucceffion of time been accumulated, or formed by the overflowing of the river.

The fecond low grounds being, in general, formed by a regular rifing of about 4 or 5 feet higher than the low lands, appears to have been originally the edge of the river. This fecond clafs or kind of land is in general extremely rich and covered with large timber and thick ftrong canes, extending in width
upon

upon an average three quarters of a mile, and in general a perfect level. It is excellent for all kinds of grain, and well calculated for the culture of indigo, hemp, flax or tobacco.

At the extremity of these second grounds, you come to what is called the high or upland, which is covered with pine, oak and hickory, and other kinds of large timber. The foil is of a good quality, but much inferior to the second or low land. It answers well for raising Indian corn, potatoes, and every thing else that delights in a dry light foil. Further out in the country again, on the West side of this river, you come to a pine barren, with extensive reed-fwamps and natural meadows or favannahs which afford excellent ranges of innumerable herds of cattle.

On the East of the river Mobille, towards the river Alabama, is one entire extended rich cane country, not inferior perhaps to any in America.

Whenever portages are made between the Mobille and Cherokee river, or their branches, which are probably but a few miles apart, the Mobille will be the first river for commerce, (the Miffiffippi excepted) in this part of the world, as it affords the shortest and most direct communication to the sea.

Sea coast between Mobille and Penfacola. The land to the eastward of Mobille Point, for about three leagues on the peninfula, is remarkable for alternate fpaces of thick and thin trees. The Point is covered with a grove of thick but not very tall ones. There is a small lagoon about four leagues to the eastward of the Point, with hardly water at the entrance for a boat, the trees about which are very tall and thick. There are feveral hillocks to the eastward along fhore, all the way from thence to the river Perdido, except at one place, about two-thirds of the way ; where double lands may be feen over a lagoon which ftretches to the weftward of that river.

River and bay of Perdido. The river Perdido empties itfelf into the fea about
10 leagues

10 leagues to the eaftward of Mobille Point, and four leagues to the weftward of the bar of Penfacola. The entrance is narrow, with a bar of fix feet; but afterwards it widens confiderably, ftretching firft to the N E upwards of a league, where it goes within a mile of the head of the great lagoon Weft of the entrance of Penfacola harbour. From this the Perdido turns to the weftward for three or four miles, where it forms a large bay. This river was formerly the boundary between Florida and Louifiana, dividing the French and Spanifh dominions.

There is nothing remarkable between the river Per- dido and the bar of Penfacola, except the grand lagoon, which reaches near to the Perdido, with fome ftraggling trees on the peninfula, and the high red bank on the North fide of it before mentioned. The foundings between the bars of Mobille and Penfacola are pretty regular, except near the bars, where there is deep water along fhore, as they ftretch out. It is neceffary in nearing them, to keep a good offing till their refpective marks are on for going over in the deepeft channel. Immediately without them there is very deep water, from 7 to 12 and 13 fathoms, oozy bottom, and good holding ground. At the fame diftance from the fhore between them, there is only fix or eight fathoms; the bottom in general is fine white fand with black fpecks and broken fhells: in fome places a coarfer bottom, and in others oozy fand.

The Weft end of the Ifland of St. Rofa ftretches athwart the mouth of the harbour, and defends it from the fea. It would be difficult to afcertain the entrance, were it not for a remarkable red cliff which not only diftinguifhes the place, but is a mark for going over the bar in the deepeft water.

The bar of Penfacola is of a femicircular form, with the convex fide to the fea, and lies at a confider-

K able

able diſtance from the land, occaſioned, no doubt, by the conflict between the ſea and the bay. The bar runs in a curve from the Weſt breakers all the way to the eaſtward of the fort, or Signal Houſe on Roſe iſland, the outer end of it extending about a mile without the breakers; it is a flat, hard ſand, but the bottom on both ſides is ſoft, oozy ground. After entering on the bar in the deepeſt channel, the old fort on Roſe iſland bears N E 1-4 N two and a half miles; the middle or higheſt red cliff, N 1-2 W three and a half miles. In coming from the eaſtward or weſtward it is beſt to keep in ſix or ſeven fathoms, till the Weſt declivity of the higheſt part of the red cliff bears about N 1-2 W, as above; and then to continue that direction. The water ſhoals gradually from four to three and three-fourths fathoms; on the ſhoaleſt part it is 21 feet, then it regularly deepens and the bottom grows ſofter.

The latitude of the bar of Penſacola is 30 d 22 m North, and longitude 87 d 40 m Weſt from London, the variation of the compaſs near 5 d Eaſt.

Directions for paſſing thro' the Bay.
When over the bar in five or ſix fathoms, it is neceſſary to incline a little towards the weſtern reef, which has deep water cloſe to it, in order to avoid the 10 feet bank that there extends about half a mile S W from the point of Roſe iſland. As the line of direction for the deepeſt water over the bar leads juſt over the Weſt point of this bank, therefore it is proper to keep within one and a half or two cables length of the breakers (on the North end of which there are two dry ſandy keys) till the Weſt point of Roſe iſland is open with the ſtraggling trees to the ſouthward of Deer Point, at the entrance of St. Roſa channel, when one muſt haul up to the eaſtward between them clear of the 10 feet bank. There is a narrow channel of 13 feet between this bank and the point of Roſe iſland. There is alſo a ſhoal ſtretching in a

ſweep

sweep from the red cliff towards the above mentioned sandy key, therefore care must be taken not to shut in Tartar Point with Deer Point; but as the soundings are regular, there is no fear, unless there be little wind, with the tide of ebb, which sets directly on this shoal, and in that case it is necessary to anchor in time.

Within Tartar Point the bay is about five or six miles broad, stretching to the North-east towards the town; which is situated on the main land, about eight miles from Rose island. From thence the bay turns more to the eastward, and is divided into two large branches or arms; one of which continues to the eastward about 18 miles from Penfacola, and the other to the northward nearly the same distance, from three to five miles broad.

Between Tartar Point and Penfacola there are two large lagoons, the southermost of which runs behind the red cliff.

All the West side of the bay, which forms a sweep towards the town, is shoal for upwards of half a mile off shore, but the soundings are regular to it. There is no danger in the bay between Penfacola and Rose island, except a shoal that runs from Deer Point, which ought to be attended to in working up or down the harbour. It is the more dangerous, as there is no warning given by the foundings; for from six fathoms, in a few casts of the lead, you have but as many feet. It runs more than half a mile to the westward from the point. The governor's house in the fort bears from the extremity of it N 1-2 E three and a half miles, and English Point N N E 1-4 E five miles. The best anchorage for large vessels is just a-breast of the town, in four fathoms, about one-third of a mile off shore; taking care not to bring the governor's house more to the westward than N W 1-4 W, on account of a shoal that runs off from

Indian

Indian Point at the East end of the town. As the tides in that offing run nearly East and West, ships should be moored accordingly.

Discovery of Penfacola. The bay of Penfacola, was first difcovered by Pamphilio de Narvaez in 1525*. After him, feveral other Spanifh adventurers vifited it, who gave it different names; as Porta da Anchufe, Bahia de St. Maria, &c. But Penfacola was the proper name of it among the Indians, which it will henceforth probably retain. The firft eftablifhment the Spaniards made here was in 1696; when Don Andrea de Arrivola was appointed governor of this province, which then comprehended a very large tract of land, on the gulph of Mexico. He built a fmall ftockado, which he called fort St. Charles, with a church, &c. juft by the red cliff at the entrance of the harbour.

This place was taken in the year 1719, by the French from Mobille. Penfacola fell at that time an eafy prey, having only about 150 men to defend it. Shortly afterwards it was retaken by the Spaniards, who were again difpoffeffed by the French in the fame year.

The fecond time the French made themfelves mafters of it, they kept poffeffion till the year 1722, when it was reftored to the crown of Spain by treaty. The Spaniards in the interim removed to St. Jofeph's bay. About the year 1726, they built a fmall town on the Weft fide of Rofe ifland, near the prefent fort, or fignal houfe, which was originally conftructed by them, but greatly improved by General Haldimand. The fettlement remained there till about the year 1754; but being then partly overflowed in a gale of wind, the town was removed to the place where it now ftands. After this country was ceded to the Englifh by the peace of 1762, many places were pointed out as conveniently

* But the Florida coaft was previoufly difcovered by Sebaftian Cabot in 1497, and by John Ponce de Leon in 1512.

veniently fituated for the purpofe of building a town; but on due examination, the prefent fituation was generally preferred, and the prefent town regularly laid out in the beginning of the year 1765.

The town of Penfacola is of an oblong form, and lies almoft parallel to the beach. It is about a mile in length, and a quarter of a mile in breadth, but contracts at both ends. At the Weft end is a fine rivulet, from which veffels are fupplied with water. The prefent fort was built by the writer of this narrative in 1775, with cedar pickets, with 4 block houfes at proper diftances, which defend or flank the works. It takes up a large fpace of ground juft in the middle of the town, which it divides in a manner into two feparate towns, and can be of no great fervice towards the defence of the place, in cafe an attack be made on it, either by the natives or a civilized enemy. *Defcription of the Town of Penfacola.*

The town of Penfacola is furrounded by two pretty large brooks of water, which take their rife under Gage hill, a fmall mount behind the town, and difcharge themfelves into the bay, one at each extremity of the town.

The town and fort of Penfacola, furrendered to the arms of his Catholic Majefty, in the year 1781, and with them the whole province of Weft Florida became fubject to the king of Spain, as before mentioned.

The hopes of a Spanifh trade induced many people to fettle here, at a great expence, but it did not anfwer their expectation. The principal objects ought to be the Indian trade, indigo, cotton, rice, hemp, tobacco and lumber, thefe being the natural produce of the country. Tho' Penfacola ftands in a very fandy fituation, yet with pains the gardens produce great plenty of vegetables. Fruit trees, fuch as orange, fig, and peach trees are here in perfection. And the bay abounds with a variety of fine fifh.

About

About a mile to the eastward of Penfacola, between it and the Englifh point, is the Eaft lagoon, which after turning to the N W 4 or 5 miles, receives the Six Mile Brook. This is a pretty little winding ftream, on the Eaft fide of which is an iron mine, where a large natural magnet was found. There is a fine mineral fpring of the Chalybeate kind, near the mouth of the lagoon, of which there are feveral others in this country.

From Englifh point, the bay ftretches to the northward. On the Weft fide, near the mouth of the river Efcambia, lies Campble Town, a fettlement of French proteftants, about 10 miles from Penfacola by land, and 13 by water. The fpot on which it ftands is high, and a very light foil; but its fituation being near to the marfhes, it is thereby rendered unhealthy, and has been the means of carrying off many of the inhabitants who were fent out in 1766, and were for fometime fupported by government, in order to manufacture filk; but either for want of proper management, or other reafons, nothing of that kind was attempted, and the place is fince abandoned and the town deftroyed.

The river Efcambia, the moft confiderable that falls into the bay of Penfacola, empties itfelf near the head of the North branch, about 12 or 15 miles from Penfacola, through feveral marfhes, and channels, which have a number of iflands between them, that are overflowed when the water is high. There is a fhoal near the entrance, and veffels that draw more than 5 or 6 feet cannot be carried into it, even through the deepeft channel; but there is from 2 to 4 fathoms afterwards. I afcended it with a boat upwards of 80 miles, where from the depth of water it appeared to be navigable for pettiaugers many miles further. It is uncertain where the fource of this river is; but fuppofed to be at a confiderable diftance, and is very winding in its courfe. The

The lands in general on each fide of the river, are rich low or fwamp, admirably adapted for the culture of rice or corn, as may fuit the planter beft; and what gives thefe low lands a fuperiority over many others, is the great number of rivulets that fall into this river from the high circumjacent country, which may eafily be led over any part of, or almoft all the rice lands, at any feafon of the year whatever. Near the mouth of this river are a great number of iflands, fome of very confiderable extent, and not inferior for rice to any in America. The fettlements made by Meffieurs Tait and Mitchell, Captain Johnfon, Mr. M'Kinnon and fome others, are very evident proofs of this affertion, who, in the courfe of two years from their firft fettlement, had nearly cleared all the expences they had been at in making very confiderable eftablifhments ; and I am well affured would entirely have done it in another year, had not the Spaniards taken poffeffion of the country.

Further up the river, we meet with other iflands, having much higher banks than thofe below, very fit for raifing Indian corn, or pulfe of all kinds, with a fufficient proportion of rice land on them alfo. The large ifland on which Mr. Marfhall made his fettlement, nearly oppofite the old ftockaded fort, about 28 miles from Penfacola by land and 40 by water, is the uppermoft ifland of any note in the river Efcambia, and is, without doubt, in point of fertility of foil, equal to any thing to be met with in the country. The wefterly part of this laft mentioned ifland is high, and not fubject to be overflown, unlefs in remarkable high frefhes, and then only fome particular low parts of it, the reft is high and well fecured againft floods; the eaftern part of it is low and liable to be overflowed at fome times of the year ; the high land extends from about a mile, to a mile and a half from the weftermoft branch of the river that furrounds it, and

is

is equal to any on the Miſſiſſippi, Amit, or Comit. A more advantageous place for ſmall ſettlements than this, is not to be met with any where near Penſacola.

The country on each ſide of the river above this iſland is higher, and as the water is confined in one channel, forms a moſt beautiful river, with great plenty of good low lands on each ſide of it for many miles up. The low lands generally extend from a mile and a half to two miles from the banks of the river, and ſome places more, when we come to a fine high pine country, intermixed with oak and hickory land. There are, on both ſides of this river, a number of riſing grounds or bluffs, which afford delightful proſpects on the river, and would be elegant ſituations for gentlemens ſeats. The low lands and iſlands abound with great quantities of white and red oak for ſtaves, which anſwer well for the Weſt-India market, and an inexhauſtible quantity of cypreſs for lumber and ſhingles, together with plenty of red and white cedar for building. The open country, or high lands bordering on theſe low rich lands are generally pine, but of a quality ſuperior to moſt other pine countries, having generally a good ſoil for five or ſix inches deep, and well adapted for raiſing corn, beans, peas, turnips, potatoes, &c.

Perhaps there is no country more beautifully diverſified with hills and dales, nor more plentifully ſupplied with fine ſtreams, than that which borders on the low lands upon this river. But what, in a very particular manner, recommends this part of Weſt-Florida, is the fine and extenſive ranges for cattle which are ſo frequently to be met with here ; it being very common for an ordinary planter to have 200 heads and ſome 1000 heads, within the vicinity of Penſacola. There is ſcarcely a ſtream in theſe parts but what has water ſufficient for ſaw-mills, and the country abounds with excellent timber for planks or lumber of all kinds.   The

The air is pure and healthy, and the planters and negroes enjoy a good ftate of health the year round. The Indians emphatically call it, on account of the fine ftreams of water every where to be met with, *the fweet water country*. Great plenty of fifh is to be found in this river, and all kinds of wild game are to be met with in great abundance.

With regard to the face of the country between the Efcambia and Penfacola, it is varied with vallies and rifing grounds. At about 20 miles from Penfacola the foil grows better than it is at the town; the vallies are covered with grafs or canes, interfperfed with thickets of laurel, myrtle, and cafina. There is generally a rivulet running through each of them, either towards the Perdido or Efcambia. The rifing grounds are chiefly covered with pines, oak, and hickory.

The North branch of the bay of Penfacola is only navigable for fmall veffels. It was formerly well fettled on each fide. The middle land between the North bay and the Ouyavalana, or Yellow Water, a branch of the Eaft bay, abounds with large tall pines fit for mafts, yards, &c.

The Yellow Water, or Middle river, enters the Middle River. Eaft branch of the bay at the N E corner, and after going about five or fix leagues up the country, the eaftern branch ends in a bafon or lake at the bottom of a rifing ground, but the weftern branch I have afcended fome leagues further. There are feveral fmall iflands near the entrance of this river, which produce cyprefs and fmall cedars, but the foil is indifferent.

The Eaft river empties into the bottom of the Eaft Eaft River. branch, about fix miles from the Middle river. It is about a quarter of a mile broad for 2 leagues, and then contracts to the breadth of 30 or 40 feet. This river comes from the eaftward, running nearly paral-

lel

lel to St. Rofes channel, and its fource is about 16 miles from its entrance into the bay.

The peninfula between the bay of Penfacola and St. Rofes channel, which is from 1 to 3 or 4 miles broad, is in general very poor fandy foil. It produces, in fome places, large pines and live oak.

Rofe Ifland. Rofe ifland extends along the coaft, for the fpace of near 50 miles, and is no where above half a mile broad. It is very remarkable for its white fandy hummocks, and ftraggling trees here and there. There is a clump of 4 tall trees clofe together, which, at a diftance, appears like one, about 18 miles from the Weft end, and another of the fame kind about a league further to the eaftward. There are likewife feveral hummocks, more eafy to remark than defcribe, but an attentive perfon, after once or twice failing along, can be at no lofs to know what part of the coaft he falls in with.

The peculiarity of the appearance of Rofe ifland from the fea, and the deep foundings all along it, are of great fervice to know the coaft: there are 9 or 10 fathoms in fome places, within a mile or two of the fhore; and, when a frigate is within 16 or 17 fathoms, the tops of the trees on the main land may be def-cried from the quarter deck. The bottom is general-ly fine white fand, with broken fhells, and black fpecks, but in one place off the Eaft end of Rofe ifland, out of fight of land, the bottom is of a coarfe gravel, mixed with coral. This ought particularly to be attended to, as it is the only fpot with that kind of foundings on the coaft: it is of a confiderable ex-tent, and there are from 20 to 30 and 40 fathoms on it, or more. There is indeed a coral bottom off the bay of Efperito Sanfto, and fome other parts on the coaft of Eaft Florida, but thefe generally begin in 7 or 8 fathoms, within fight of land; from which and the difference of latitude, one cannot be mifta-ken for the other.   This

This is a very extensive bay, stretching about 30 Bay of St. Rosa. miles to the north-east, and is from 4 to 6 miles broad. There is a bar before it with only 7 or 8 feet where deepest. But afterwards there is 16 or 17 feet, as far as the red bluff on the main land. The channel between this bluff and the East part of Rose island is but narrow, and a little further on, towards the bay, it is choaked up with a large shoal in some places dry, the deepest water on it is only 4 or 5 feet; so that nothing but very small vessels can enter this bay from the sea, and the channel between Rose island and the main, is just sufficient for boats or pettiaugers.

On the North side of St. Rose's bay, almost opposite to the entrance from the sea, there are three pretty large branches, which stretch several miles: the westermost, which is the largest, is again subdivided into smaller branches, all which have deep water. The other two receive each a considerable rivulet of clear water with a rapid stream. On the banks there is plenty of cedar, &c.

The largest river that falls into St. Rose's bay is the Chacta-hatcha River. Chacta-hatcha or Pea river, which runs from the N E, and enters the bottom of the bay through several mouths, but so shoal that only a small boat or canoe can pass them. I ascended this river about 25 leagues, where there is settled a small party of the Couffac Indians. The banks of this river, in point of soil and timber, resembles very much those of the river Escambia.

Between the bays of St. Rosa, and St. Andrews, Coast between the bays of St. Rosa and St. Andrews. the coast runs E S E, and S E by E, for the space of 52 miles, the soundings much the same as off Rose island; it is to be observed that the trees are thick, and come pretty close to the shore. There are likewise some red hummocks as well as white, which with the trenching of the land may be of service to know that part of the coast. The

St. Andrew's
Bay.

The entrance of St. Andrew's bay is between a
small island on the right hand, and a narrow peninsula on the left. There is a high white sand hill,
which is a remarkable object from the sea: it lies in
latitude 30 d 06 m North, and about 10 leagues to
the North-west of Cape Blaise. From the point of the
peninsula, there is a large shoal extending for more
than two thirds of the way towards the island; which
is 2 miles distant, leaving a channel of 17 or 18 feet,
but it has a small bar of 13 feet.

There is anchorage just within St. Andrew's island
in 3 fathoms and an half, but it is more commodi-
ous within the point of the peninsula in 5 fathoms,
with the advantage of fresh water, which is easily got
by digging.

St. Andrew's bay runs first to the N W, nearly
parallel to the sea shore, for 3 leagues; then it turns
to the eastward for about a league, when a large
branch breaks off to the S E. The main body continues to the northward for 2 leagues, when it is divided into two large branches, one going to the N E,
and the other to the westward. This last, which is the
least, reaches within a few miles of St. Rosa's bay.
The country between them is low and marshy, and full
of fresh water ponds.

St. Andrew's bay is navigable for any vessels that
can go over the bar. There is a large shoal with only
3 or 4 feet, about half way up the first reach, but
there is a deep channel on the West side of it, and afterwards there is from 3 to 7 fathoms all over the bay.
There are no rivers of any consequence, nor can the
soil immediately on the bay be much commended;
there is however great plenty of large pines, live oak,
and cedar.

Coast from St.
Andrew's
island to the
bay of St.
Joseph.

From St. Andrew's island to the bay of St. Joseph's,
the middle of the coast between them runs about E
S E near 15 miles, with a shoal all the way between
them

them near the shore, which easily appears, it being of
a whiteish colour. There is from 12 to 18 feet on
the greatest part of it, except towards the mouth of
St. Joseph's bay, where there is a bank near the
middle, between St. Joseph's point and the main land,
with only 7 or 8 feet, and 4 fathoms just within;
but there is a very good channel with 3 fathoms on
the bar, between that bank and St. Joseph's point,
on the right hand going in.

In going into St. Joseph's bay it is requisite to keep St. Joseph's
within a cable and a half or two cables length of the Bay.
peninsula, in five or four and a half fathoms, as it
shoals regularly towards the point, from which a spit
of sand runs out a little way ; and when in three fathoms to haul round gradually, still keeping near
two cables length off shore. The bar is narrow, and
immediately within it there is from four to six and a
half fathoms soft ground. The end of the peninsula
forms two or three points, from each of which a small
spit runs off for a little distance, which may be known
by the discoloured water on them. This is an excellent harbour ; in which the best place for anchoring is just within the peninsula, opposite to some ruins
that still remain of the village of St. Joseph. There
the Spaniards had a post, which they abandoned a-
bout the year 1700, but they took possession of it
again in 1719. There is very good water to be got
here by digging, and on the North side of the bay
are two or three small fresh water brooks, opposite
to which are three or four fathoms close to the shore.
In the year 1717, the French erected a fort which
they called Crœvcœur, a mile to the northward of
a brook in St. Joseph's bay, opposite to the point of
the peninsula, but abandoned in the next year, on
the representation of the governor of Pensacola that
it belonged to his Catholic Majesty. The bay is nearly of the figure of a horse-shoe, being about twelve

miles in length, and feven acrofs where broadeft. Towards the bottom of it are a few fmall iflands, and
the water is fo fhoal that a boat can hardly go near
the fhore.

The foil on the North fide of the bay is very fandy,
but there are fome fpots near the ruins of St. Jofeph's
that are covered with a kind of verdure, and produce
plenty of grapes, fome of which are large, of a pur-
ple colour, and pretty good to the tafte : they were
probably planted there by the Spaniards. There are
here likewife fome fmall cabbage trees, of which there
are great numbers on St. George's iflands beyond Cape
Blaife, and on all the coaft to the eaftward. Thefe
cabbage trees do not grow above the height of 20
feet ; the bud, or unformed leaves in the heart being
boiled has fomewhat the tafte of cabbage, but is
more delicious.

A very good eftablifhment might be made here for
a fifhery, as the fettlers might make falt on the fpot
to cure the bafs, rock, cod, grouper, red mullet, and
other kinds of fifh, which are here in great abundance ; and, when well cured, are little if at all inferior to thofe brought from the northward.

Peninfula be-
tween St. Jo-
feph's and
Cape Blaife.
The peninfula between St. Jofeph's and Cape Blaife
is a narrow flip of land, in fome places not above a
quarter of a mile broad. The gaps here and there
upon it, and the water in the bay appearing through
them from the maft-head, together with the trenching of the land about NNW, and SSE, for near four
leagues, make it eafily known. The trees about Cape
Blaife are very thick, and there is a remarkable fingle
tree, like a bufh, that ftands without the others towards the point. In cafe of an eafterly wind, there
is fafe anchorage oppofite the thickeft trees in fix or
feven fathoms, about one or two miles off fhore ; and
there is a large pond of frefh water near the beach,
about three or four miles to the eaftward of Cape
Blaife.

Blaife. There is alfo a remarkable gap among the trees between the fea and the bottom of St. Jofeph's bay, where is a narrow ifthmus not above 5 or 600 yards broad.

Cape Blaife, where it ends in a low point near two miles from the trees, in latitude 29 d 40 m N, is not only remarkable from the aforefaid circumftances, but likewife on account of the irregular foundings that are found a great way out at fea from it. There is a fpit of land that runs about two miles from the point in a SSE direction ; and there are feveral banks of three or four fathoms, at the diftance of fix or feven miles, with deep water from feven to ten fathoms between them. There are even fome banks of five and fix fathoms almoft out of fight of land from the maft-head; but though they may alarm a ftranger, there is no danger in going near enough to make the land plain.

There is another cape or point of land about fix leagues to the eaftward of Cape Blaife, being an elbow of the largeft of St. George's iflands, nearly oppofite to the river Apalachicola. This point lies in 29 d 38 m N. There is a large fhoal running out from it a confiderable way, but how far has not yet been afcertained. The coaft between it and Cape Blaife forms a kind of hollow bay, with deep foundings and a foft bottom. There are two iflands to the North-weft of St. George's cape ; that neareft to it is fmall, and remarkable for a clump of ftraggling trees on the middle of it ; the other is a pretty large ifland of a triangular form, and reaches within three leagues of Cape Blaife, having a paffage at each end of it for fmall craft into the bay, between thefe iflands and the river Apalachicola : but this bay is full of fhoals and oyfter banks, and not above two or three feet water at moft in any of the branches of that river.

Having thus given an account of the fea-coaft of Weft-

Weft-Florida, I fhall conclude with a few general obfervations on the feafons, winds, tides, &c. As moft of the bars lie a confiderable way without the entrance of the bays and rivers, the water feldom rifes or falls on them above a foot; but in the bays or channels it rifes two or three feet. The tides are irregular, and feem to be governed in a great meafure by the winds; but not always by that wind which blows directly on the fpot. Though there is generally about 12 hours flood and 12 hours ebb, yet it often happens that there are two tides of each in the fpace of 24 hours; and fometimes the tide will run one way for the fpace of 18 hours together, and only five or fix hours the contrary, fo that nothing can be faid with certainty on this fubject. By reafon of the trade winds blowing in the Atlantic ocean, and continuing into the bay of Mexico, it is natural to fuppofe that the water, being there hemmed in, will of courfe force a paffage out where it finds the leaft refiftance; which is through the gulph 'of Florida. From this general principle it fhould follow, that on the coaft of Weft-Florida it ought to run from Weft to Eaft, which in fome meafure would account for the fhoals being found at the Eaft end of all the iflands on this coaft, and deep water on the Weft ends; but in a large bay or Mediterranean fea like that of Mexico, where there are fo many rivers, bays, &c. the general courfe of the current muft be greatly difturbed. From this proceeds that irregularity which is obfervable on the North fide of the bay of Mexico, where the tide of ebb always fets to the eaftward near the fhore, and the flood from the fouthward or S E: what it may do in the offing has not yet been examined, nor will it be eafily determined.

To the eaftward of Cape Blaife, the general obfervations concerning the deep water at the Weft end of
the

the iflands and peninfulas, and vice verfa, do not feem always to hold good. Indeed, as far as has been examined of the Weft part of Eaft-Florida, it is a fhoal a confiderable way from the land, (and therefore ought to be known only to be avoided) except the bay of Efperitu Sancto*, at the entrance of which, in the latitude 27 d 8 m, there is four fathoms and fafe anchorage.

From the winds that prevail in general on this coaft during the months of April, May, and to the middle of June, the weather is mild. The fea and land breezes are pretty regular, and they generally continue fo all the fummer. In July, Auguft, and moft of September, there are frequent fqualls, with much rain, thunder, and lightning ; and fometimes gales of wind from the South and South-weft for feveral days together. From the middle of October to the end of March, the northerly winds prevail, which at times blow very hard during that feafon ; when the wind changes to the eaftward or fouthward of that point, it is commonly attended with clofe, hazy, or foggy weather.

It ought to be obferved in failing in the Gulph of Mexico, to be very careful of logs or driftwood in the night time ; for when the waters of the Miffiffippi are high, that river difgorges an immenfe number of large logs, or trees, which being driven by the winds and currents all over the gulph, may do confiderable damage to veffels under full fail.

M I fhall

* The bay of Efperitu Sancto is fituated on the Weft coaft of the province of Eaft-Florida, in 27 deg. of North latitude. It has a good harbour, but the land all about that coaft is very low, and cannot be feen from a fhip's deck when in feven fathoms water. Several low fandy iflands and marfhes, covered with mangrove bufhes, lie before the main land. Here is the greateft quantity of fifh in the fummer time imaginable, which may be catched with a feine, enough to load a fhip, if the climate would admit of curing them, even in a few days.

Here is ftone proper for building, on this coaft. Alfo great plenty of deer, and fome wild cattle. But the main land near the coaft is in general fandy and barren, and is intermixed in many places with vallies capable of improvement for ftock of all forts. The bay and iflands before the main land abound with fifh and various forts of wild fowl.

I SHALL here subjoin some Remarks on the Tortugas, &c. as heretofore published by George Gauld, Esquire.

AS a competent knowledge of the situation of the Dry Tortugas is absolutely necessary for the navigation to and from the North side of the bay of Mexico, and from the West-Indies through the Gulph of Florida, a few general remarks concerning them may not be unacceptable to the public at this time.

They consist of ten small islands, or keys, extending E N E and W S W for ten or eleven miles, at the distance of about thirty leagues from the nearest part of the coast of Florida, forty from the island of Cuba; and fourteen leagues from the westermost of the Florida keys. They are all very low, but some of them covered with mangrove bushes, and may be seen at four leagues distance. The southwestermost keys, which, in going from Pensacola, Mobille, or the Mississippi, is the corner to be turned, and coming from Cape Antonio the point to be avoided, lies in 24 d 32 m North latitude, and about 83 d 50 m West longitude, from the Royal Observatory at Greenwich; the variation of the compass, by a medium of several observations, is seven degrees East. A reef of coral rocks runs about a quarter of a mile S W from these keys, the water on which is discoloured; and in general, wherever there is danger it may easily be seen from the mast-head in the day time. There is a large bank of brown coral rocks, intermixed with white patches of sand, about five or six miles to the westward of the Tortugas, with very irregular soundings from six to twelve fathoms; the bottom appears very plainly, and though it may be alarming to strangers, yet there is no danger. You will find from thirteen to seventeen fathoms between this bank and the Tortugas.   If

If you are bound to the eaftward, and meet with a ftrong eafterly gale, which is frequent there in the fummer feafon, you may fafely come to an anchor in five or fix fathoms, under the lee of the long fandy ifland to the northward of the S W key, about a quarter of a mile off fhore. The bank of foundings extends only about five or fix leagues to the fouthward of the Tortugas, but much farther to the weftward, and all the way to the northward along the Florida fhore. This is a lucky circumftance for the fafety of navigation in thofe parts, as caution in foundings may prevent any danger in the night time; for the foundings are extremely regular all along this bank to the northward, almoft to Cape Blaife, in latitude 29 d 41 m : fo that by the latitude and depth of water, we generally know how far we are to the eaftward or weftward. There is a fpace of feveral leagues together, from twenty to fifty fathoms, but from fifty or fixty it deepens faft to feventy, eighty, and foon after no ground.

From the bar of Penfacola to the Dry Tortugas the true courfe is S 30 d E 134 leagues, and therefore SE by S by the compafs will carry you clear of them to the weftward ; but it will be both prudent and neceffary to found frequently when you get into the latitude of 26 d and 25 m, and never ftand in to lefs than thirty fathoms in the night time, till you are paft the latitude of 24 d 30 m, when you may haul up S E by E or E S E, which will carry you near to the Havanna.

There is a broad channel over the bank to the eaftward of the Tortugas, of ten to feventeen fathoms, which, in going to and from the coaft of Weft-Florida, &c. might occafionally cut off a great deal of the diftance ; but that paffage is by no means to be attempted, unlefs you can fee the Tortugas diftinctly, and keep within two or three leagues of the
eaftermoft

eaftermoft of them, as there is a coral bank of only twelve feet at the diftance of five leagues, and farther on towards Cayo Marques, the weftermoft of the Florida keys, there is a very dangerous and extenfive bank of quickfand, on many parts of which there are no more than four or five feet of water. It is of a remarkable white colour, and may be eafily feen and avoided in the day time.

HAVING now finifhed my intended narrative, I fhall clofe it with the following obfervations upon the probable confequences that will arife to the United States of America, from the poffeffion of fo extenfive a country, abounding with fuch a variety of climate, foil, and productions; referring my reader for his further information upon the fubject, to the Philofophical Effays publifhed in London in 1772, concerning the ftate of the Britifh empire on this continent.

There is fome amufement at leaft in reflecting upon the vaft confequences, which fome time or other muft infallibly attend the fettling of America. If we confider the progrefs of the empires which have hitherto exifted in the world, we fhall find the fhort duration of their moft glorious periods, owing to caufes which will not operate againft that of North America. Thofe empires were formed by conqueft; a great many nations different in character, language and ideas, were by force jumbled into one heterogeneous power: it is moft furprifing that fuch diffonant parts fhould hold together fo long. But when the band of union was weakened, they returned to their original and natural feparation: language and national character formed many fovereignties out of the former connected varieties. This, however, will be very different with North America. The habitable parts of which, including the dominions of Britain

and

and of Spain, North of latitude 30d, contain above
3,500,000 fquare miles. It would be unneceffary to
remark, that this includes what at prefent docs not
belong to our North America. If we want it, I
warrant it will foon be ours. This extent of terri-
tory is much greater than that of any empire that
ever exifted, as will appear by the following table.

Square Miles.

The Perfian empire under Darius con-
    tained -   -   -   -   1,650,000
The Roman empire in its utmoft extent 1,610,000
The Chinefe empire, -   -   -   -   1,749,000
The Great Mogul's, - - - -   1,116,000

The Ruffian empire, including all Tartary, is larger
than any of thefe. But I might as well throw into
the American fcale the countries about the Hudfon's
bay, for the one is as likely to be peopled as the o-
ther; whereas all I have taken in will affuredly be fo.
Befides, North-America is actually peopling very faft,
which is far enough from being the cafe with the
Ruffian deferts. Now the habitable part of what was
once the Britifh dominions alone in North-America,
contains above 1,200,000 fquare miles, or almoft
equal to any of the above. But the whole, as I before obferved, is 3,500,000, or more than the Perfian and Roman empires together. In refpect, therefore, to extent, and the means of maintaining numbers of people, it is fuperior to all. But then comes
the advantage which is decifive of its duration. This
immenfe continent will be peopled by perfons whofe
language and national character muft be the fame.
Foreigners who may refort to us, will be confounded
by the general population, and the whole people, phy-
fically fpeaking, one: fo that thofe feeds of decay,
fown in the very foundation of the ancient empires,
will

will have no exiftence here. Further, the peopling of this vaft tract from a nation renowned in trade, navigation and naval power, has occafioned all the ideas of the original to be tranfplanted into the copy. And thefe advantages having been fo long enjoyed, with the amazing and unparalleled fituation for commerce between Europe, Afia, and the great fouthern continent ; and America at the fame time poffeffing, above other countries, the means of building, fitting out, and maintaining a great navy ; the inhabitants of this potent empire, fo far from being in the leaft danger from the attacks of any other quarter of the globe, will have it in their power to engrofs the whole commerce of it, and to reign, not only lords of America, but to poffefs, in the utmoft fecurity, the dominion of fea throughout the world, which their anceftors enjoyed before them. None of the ancient empires, therefore, which fell a prey to the Tartars, nor the prefent one of China, can be compared to this of North-America, which, as furely as the land is now in being, will hereafter be trod by the firft people the world ever knew.

F I N I S.

E R R A T A.

TABLE OF DISTANCES.

	Miles.
From the Balize or the Mouths of the Miſſiſſippi	
to the Detour aux Plaquemines, is - -	32
to beginning of the ſettlements - - -	20
to the Detour des Anglois - - -	35
to New Orleans - - - -	18
to the villages of the Humas and Alibama Indians - - - - -	60
to the Fourche de Chetimachas and Indian village of the ſame name - -	3
to the Conceſſion of Monſ. Paris - -	9
to the Ibberville - - - -	27
to Baton Rouge - - - -	18
to the ſettlement of Point Coupeé -	17
to upper end of this ſettlement where there is a village of Tunica Indians on the Eaſt ſide - - - - -	20
to the Chafalaya, the uppermoſt mouth of the Miſſiſſippi - - - -	30
to the River Rouge - - - -	3
to Fort Roſalie at the Natchez - -	56
to the Petit Goufre - - -	31 ¼
to the Grand Goufre - - -	14
to the Yazou Cliffs - - -	39 ¾
to the River Yazou - - - -	7 ½
to the River Arkanſaw - - -	158 ¼
to the River St. Francis - - -	108
to the River and Heights of Margot -	70 ½
to the Chickaſaw River - - -	104 ½
to Mine au fer - - - -	67 ½
to the River Ohio - - - -	15
Total,	964 ½

www.ingramcontent.com/pod-product-compliance
Lightning Source LLC
Chambersburg PA
CBHW021410090426
42742CB00009B/1085